JESUS, THE FINAL DAYS

JESUS, THE FINAL DAYS

What Really Happened

CRAIG A. EVANS and N. T. WRIGHT

Edited by Troy A. Miller

WESTMINSTER
JOHN KNOX PRESS
LOUISVILLE · KENTUCKY

Published in the United States of America by Westminster John Knox Press in 2009 as
Jesus, the Final Days: What Really Happened

Published in Great Britain in 2008 as *Jesus, the Final Days* by the Society for
Promoting Christian Knowledge, 36 Causton Street, London, SW1P 4ST

First edition
Westminster John Knox Press
Louisville, Kentucky

09 10 11 12 13 14 15 16 17 18—10 9 8 7 6 5 4 3 2

Book design by Drew Stevens
Cover design by Jennifer K. Cox

Library of Congress Cataloging-in-Publication Data

Evans, Craig A.
  Jesus, the final days : what really happened / Craig A. Evans & N. T. Wright ; edited
by Troy A. Miller.—1st ed.
    p. cm.
  Includes index.
  ISBN 978-0-664-23359-4 (alk. paper)
  1. Jesus Christ—Passion. 2. Jesus Christ—Resurrection. I. Wright, N. T. (Nicholas
Thomas) II. Miller, Troy A. III. Title.
  BT431.3.E93 2008
  232.96—dc22   2008018543

PRINTED IN THE UNITED STATES OF AMERICA

♾ The paper used in this publication meets the minimum requirements
of the American National Standard for Information Sciences—Permanence
of Paper for Printed Library Materials, ANSI Z39.48-1992

Westminster John Knox Press advocates the responsible use of our natural resources.
The text paper of this book is made from 30% post-consumer waste.

CONTENTS

PREFACE

Often in matters of Scripture and theology, the gap between the academy on one side and the church on the other is wide—often, regretfully, too wide. The academy is deemed to be only about the business of thought, argument, and mental reflection—the proverbial ivory tower. In contrast, the church is held to be the locale of praxis or the doing of the Christian faith, as seen in worship, evangelism, faith formation, and prayer. This separation and dichotomy, though real in how it is reinforced by some parties in each of these entities, is artificial. It does not reflect the rich and diverse contributions that have emerged from the church and the academy through the ages; nor does it echo how they both have been vital to promoting and sustaining an orthodox and incarnational Christian faith. What is needed in today's age is for Christians to continue to create arenas in which mutual edification can occur—arenas in which the best of what the church and the academy have to offer can be brought together in conversation, learning, and mission for the glory of God.

The three chapters that make up this brief book first took shape as lectures in the Symposium for Church and Academy lecture series at Crichton College. As the director of the larger Symposium for Church and Academy initiative, I created and developed this lecture series to begin to redress the gap or separation noted above and to establish covenantal relationships between the Department of Bible and Theology at Crichton and local area churches for the purpose of mutual edification and shared ministry. Those sought as speakers for this series were persons who brought a first-rate, international reputation for scholarship in matters of Scripture or theology, as well as a demonstrable commitment to and participation in the gospel mission of the Christian church. Auspiciously, N. T. Wright (2003) and Craig A. Evans (2004) accepted the invitation to come as the first two lecturers in this new series. They have been followed in subsequent years by others, such as Gordon Fee, Maxie Dunnam, and Dennis Hollinger.

The present book comprises two of Craig's lectures (one each on Jesus' death and burial) and one of Tom's lectures (on Jesus' resurrection) that have been revised for publication for a wider audience. As both of their lecture topics focused on the life of Jesus, the selected lectures fell neatly into place. Beyond the subject matter of Jesus' life, the essays in the book also share a common focus or intent. Both of the authors examine events in Jesus' life from a historical perspective with the aim of reviewing the pertinent evidence so as to surmise what really did (or in some cases most likely did) happen. Craig and Tom, along with most Christians, recognize that determining what actually happened is vitally important to the validity of the Christian faith. Though not equal to each other, history is of vital importance for faith. What really happened does matter!

Finally, in attempting to discern historical matters related to Jesus' death, burial, and resurrection, the chapters also share, almost by necessity, an apologetic edge. While engaging in apologetics is not at the forefront of the authors' intent, any thorough evaluation of historical issues related to a given event necessitates the examination of other historical theories or claims already out there, and this book is no exception. Therefore, in their effort to present as historically accurate a recounting as possible for these events in Jesus' life, the authors also at times lend confirmation to current theories that reinforce their findings and at other times expose hypotheses or claims that lack historical credibility.

This book, though not entirely uninformative for the scholar of the New Testament, Jesus, or late Second Temple Judaism, is intended for a wider readership—for the interested layperson, for clergy, for the undergraduate or graduate student, as well as for those who have academic specialties outside of one of these areas. We hope that the book will be read in the academy and the church, and that it will provoke thought, reflection, learning, and a thoroughgoing life of faith.

Projects such as this do not come about without a great deal of support and guidance. I would first like to say thank you to the leadership of Crichton College for supporting my vision for the Symposium for Church and Academy. I would also like to thank the Episcopal Diocese of West Tennessee, the Wilberforce Education Foundation, Trinity Baptist Church (Cordova, Tennessee), and Crichton College for the monetary support they provided for the lecture series in which Tom and Craig participated. I would like to thank our editor at Westminster John Knox Press, Philip Law, for helping field and shepherd along the book. Thanks is also due to my student Nathan Brasfield, who helped prepare the indexes. Finally, I wish to express my gratitude to N. T. Wright and Craig Evans, not only for their participation in this project as lecturers and authors, but also for their accompanying kindness, humility, and friendship. Your faith in Jesus needs no words to be seen and heard.

Troy A. Miller
Easter 2008
Memphis, Tennessee

ABBREVIATIONS

1 Macc	*1 Maccabees*
2 Bar	*2 Baruch*
2 Macc	*2 Maccabees*
4 Macc	*4 Maccabees*
Ant.	Josephus's *Jewish Antiquities*
Augustus	Suetonius's *Life of Augustus*
b. Megillah	Babylonian Talmud, *Megillah*
b. Qiddushin	Babylonian Talmud, *Qiddushin*
Caligula	Suetonius's *Life of Caligula*
CIL	*Corpus Inscriptionum Latinarum*
Hist. Alex.	Curtius Rufus's *History of Alexander*
Hist. Eccl.	Eusebius's *Ecclesiastical History*
In Flaccum	Philo's *Against Flaccus*
J.W.	Josephus's *Jewish War*
Jub.	*Jubilees*
Lev. Rab.	*Leviticus Rabbah*
m. Pesahim	Mishnah, *Pesahim*
m. Sanhedrin	Mishnah, *Sanhedrin*
Mek.	*Mekilta*
Mor.	Plutarch's *Moralia*
Nat. Hist.	Pliny the Elder's *Natural History*
P.Florence	Florence Papyri
P.Louvre	Louvre Papyri
Pompey	Plutarch's *Life of Pompey*

Ps.-Manetho	Pseudo-Manetho
Ps.-Philo, *Bib. Ant.*	Pseudo-Philo's *Biblical Antiquities*
Ps.-Quintilian	Pseudo-Quintilian
Qoh. Rab.	*Qoheleth Rabbah*
Sipre Num.	Sifre, Numbers
t. Menah.	Tosefta, *Menahot*
T. Moses	*Testament of Moses*
Verr.	Cicero's *In Verrem*
y. Moe'ed Qatan	Jerusalem Talmud, *Moe'ed Qatan*

Chapter One
THE SHOUT OF DEATH
Craig A. Evans

The earliest formal creed, or confession of faith, of the
Christian church is the Apostles' Creed, which probably
came to expression in the third century. The familiar creed
reads:

> I believe in God, the Father Almighty,
> Maker of heaven and earth.
> And in Jesus Christ, his only Son, our Lord;
> Who was conceived by the Holy Spirit,
> Born of the Virgin Mary;
> Suffered under Pontius Pilate,
> was crucified, dead and buried;
> He descended into Hades;
> The third day he rose from the dead;
> He ascended into heaven;
> and sits at the right hand of God the Father Almighty;
> From thence he shall come to judge the living
>   and the dead.
> I believe in the Holy Spirit;
> the holy catholic Church;
> the communion of saints;
> the forgiveness of sins;
> the resurrection of the body;
> and the life everlasting. Amen.

The heart of the creed is found in its middle, where of Jesus it is said: "Suffered under Pontius Pilate, was crucified, dead and buried. He descended into Hades; The third day he rose from the dead." This part of the creed draws upon and summarizes much earlier statements of Christian faith, many of which are found in the New Testament writings themselves. One example from the middle of the first century is found in a letter by the apostle Paul. Speaking of the gospel Paul affirms, "For I handed on to you as of first importance what I in turn had received: that Christ died for our sins in accordance with the scriptures, and that he was buried, and that he was raised on the third day in accordance with the scriptures, and that he appeared to Cephas, then to the twelve" (1 Cor. 15:3–5).

The present book is concerned with the three essential elements of this creed: the death, burial, and resurrection of Jesus. It should hardly surprise anyone that the most often doubted and attacked element is the third one, the belief in the resurrection of Jesus. But in recent years it also has become quite fashionable to raise objections against the first two elements, against the historical reality of his death and burial.

The firm conviction of the authors of this book is that behind the creed, behind the faith claims of the Christian movement, is history. The death, burial, and resurrection of Jesus are not merely theological ideas but actual events—actual events that awakened faith and later prompted theological inquiry. In this first chapter we begin by taking a closer look at the death of Jesus, an event, ironically enough, that initially did anything but awaken faith.

THE REALITY OF THE DEATH OF JESUS

No serious historian of any religious or nonreligious stripe doubts that Jesus of Nazareth really lived in the first century and was executed under the authority of Pontius Pilate, the governor of Judea and Samaria. Though this may be common knowledge among scholars, the public may well not be aware of this. Objections, though, still persist. In fact, a recent book has recycled the odd notion that Jesus wasn't really executed but actually faked his death, with the assistance of the Roman governor and a few others, and then fled to Egypt. Proof of this assertion, it is claimed, is found in two letters said to be written in Aramaic and alleged to have been found under a house in Jerusalem forty years ago. These writings are alleged to be carefully preserved by a collector whose name cannot be revealed and who lives in a city that cannot be disclosed. Of course, neither the author of this fantasy nor the owner of these letters can read Aramaic or possesses the requisite expertise to verify ancient writings. Regrettably, the utter silliness of this scenario escapes many in today's reading public.

The death of Jesus is not only affirmed (or at least presupposed) in every writing of the New Testament and early Christianity, it is attested by early Jewish and Roman writers as well. Josephus, a first-century Jewish historian, apologist, and survivor of the catastrophic rebellion against Rome (AD 66–70), states that Jesus, having been accused by the Jewish leaders, was condemned to the cross by Pilate (*Ant.* 18.63–64). According to the Roman historian Tacitus, "Christ . . . suffered the death penalty during the reign of Tiberius, by sentence of the procurator Pontius Pilate" (*Annals* 15.44). Although Tacitus errs slightly in upgrading Pilate's rank (he was a prefect, not a procurator), his terse summary agrees with what we find in Josephus and in the Christian Gospels. Lucian of Samosata, in a mocking reference to Peregrinus and the Christians with whom for a time he associated, refers to Jesus as "the man who was crucified in Palestine" (*Passing of Peregrinus* §11; cf. §13 "that crucified sophist"). Finally, Mar bar Serapion, a Syrian, in a letter written to his son perhaps toward the end of the first century, makes reference to the death of Jesus, the Jewish "wise king."

The reality of the death of Jesus also finds confirmation in the simple fact that it was not anticipated by his followers. When Jesus spoke of his impending suffering and death, Peter, spokesperson for the disciples, took his master aside and rebuked him (Mark 8:31–33), a sure sign of Peter's lack of this expectation. What then did they expect? They expected to sit at Jesus' right and left, that is, to form Israel's new government (Matt. 19:28; Mark 10:35–40; Luke 22:28–30). The kingdom (or rule) of God had dawned, and the rule of Satan was coming to an end (Mark 1:15; 3:11, 22–27; Luke 10:17–19; 11:20). How then did the martyrdom of God's Chosen One fit into this picture?

The death of Jesus actually was a source of embarrassment for Jesus' early followers. It is to this embarrassment that Paul alludes when he declares that he is "not ashamed of the gospel" (Rom. 1:16). In the thinking of the Roman world, sons of God, heroes, and saviors did not die on crosses. In that time, there was no sentimentality attached to Jesus' death and certainly not to the cross, a horrifying symbol in Roman antiquity. In what way any of this could be termed "good news" (the meaning of the word "gospel") would be far from clear to Jews and Gentiles alike.

Had Jesus not been executed, had Jesus not been crucified, why make up such a preposterous story?

No, the death of Jesus is no fiction. It was a grim historical reality. It was known to non-Christians, and it was a demoralizing event for Jesus' followers—at least initially—and an ongoing embarrassment as the church proclaimed Jesus as Savior and Son of God throughout the Roman Empire. There can be no doubt that Jesus was executed. But why?

THE REASONS FOR THE DEATH OF JESUS

Many people, including Christians, do not know why Jesus was executed, why he encountered deadly opposition. I have heard people say that Jesus was put to death because he was a good man or because hypocritical Pharisees feared him. This really, though, is the stuff of nonsense. The New Testament Gospels reveal several historical factors, all near the end of Jesus' life, that led to his execution; his goodness and his quarrels with Pharisees were not among them.

The first reason that Jesus aroused opposition was because of the manner of his entry into Jerusalem at the beginning of the final week of his ministry. He entered the holy city mounted on a donkey, amid shouts of "Hosanna! Blessed is the coming kingdom of our ancestor David!" (Mark 11:1–10; here vv. 9–10, NRSV, modified). Entering the city in this way deliberately mimicked Solomon, David's son, who one thousand years earlier rode the royal mule as part of his declaration of kingship (1 Kgs. 1:32–40). Such an entry also answered the ancient prophecy of the anticipated humble king (Zech. 9:9). Not only did Jesus' act recall hopes of a coming son of David,

but the crowd's response reflected the same popular interpretation of it. Their Hosannas, as an allusion to Psalm
118, were a pronouncement that this one who comes to the
temple "in the name of the Lord" is none other than David,
the one destined to be Israel's king and ruler (see Ps.
118:19–27, according to the Aramaic paraphrase). Such an
event suggested in unmistakable terms that Israel's king
was Jesus, not Caesar. Thus, from the very moment of entry
into Jerusalem, Jesus was set on a collision course with
Roman authority.

The second reason that Jesus aroused opposition
was because of his actions in the temple precincts or
grounds. His well-known action here disrupted sacrificial
trade and traffic and challenged the ruling priests with very
troubling words (Mark 11:15–18):

> "Is it not written,
> 'My house shall be called a house of prayer for
>   all the nations'?
> But you have made it a 'cave of robbers.'"
> (v. 17, NRSV, modified)

The first part of these words is a quotation taken from
Isaiah 56:7, part of an oracle that looks forward to the day
when all peoples, Gentiles and Jews from afar, will come to
Jerusalem and will be welcome. All peoples will worship
the God of Israel; their gifts will be received and their
prayers will be heard. This oracle expressed nothing new
for Jews at that time; it reflects the original purpose for the
temple, as reflected in Solomon's ancient prayer of dedication (1 Kgs. 8:41–43). Jesus' action and his questioning
appeal to Isaiah's oracle implies that the temple authorities
have failed to live up to their calling. The temple has not

become a place of prayer for the nations. Rather, it has become a "cave of robbers." Here in the second part Jesus alludes to Jeremiah's scathing criticism of the temple establishment of his day (Jer. 7:11), warning that God will destroy the temple. The ruling priests, scribes, and elders would have been deeply offended by Jesus' critical and offensive words.

That preaching angry sermons based on Jeremiah 7 could get one into trouble is attested in Josephus. Josephus tells us of one Jesus ben Ananias, who beginning in AD 62 began prophesying the doom of the city of Jerusalem and her famous temple. Like Jesus of Nazareth, Jesus ben Ananias alluded to Jeremiah 7, while in the vicinity of the temple (Josephus, *J.W.* 6.300–305; cf. Jer. 7:34). This later Jesus was lucky. Unlike Jesus of Nazareth, Jesus ben Ananias was not executed (despite calls from religious leaders that he be put to death), but was released. However, his luck ran out seven years later when, during a siege, Jesus ben Ananias was killed by a catapult stone that came hurtling over the walls.

The third reason that Jesus aroused opposition was his telling of the parable of the Vineyard (Mark 12:1–12). He narrated this parable as an indirect answer to the question put to him by the ruling priests and their supporters, who demanded to know by what authority Jesus did what he had done in the temple precincts (Mark 11:27–33). It is bad enough that Jesus based his parable on Isaiah's parable of the Vineyard, which warned Israel of impending judgment because of its failure to pursue justice (Isa. 5:1–7). What made Jesus' parable particularly annoying to the ruling priests was that Isaiah's parable had come to be understood as primarily directed against the temple establishment. We see this perspective in the Aramaic paraphrase of Isaiah 5, in later rabbinic interpretation, and in a scroll from Qumran (4Q500) that dates to the first century BC. Jesus' point was hard to miss: because of their rebellion against God, especially as seen in their plotting to murder his own Son, the ruling priests face judgment. This threat, together with the implied threat earlier when Jesus appealed to Jeremiah 7, prompted the ruling priests to seek Jesus' life.

The fourth reason that Jesus aroused opposition was his anointing by the unnamed woman (Mark 14:3–9). For years commentators were reluctant to interpret this act as a messianic anointing on the part of the woman, suggesting instead that it was a Passover holiday anointing, akin perhaps to today's Christmas mistletoe. This scholarly reluctance was probably due to the faulty assumption by some that Jesus did not understand himself in messianic terms. This odd notion has been seriously challenged of late, not least because of the discovery of a scroll from Qumran (4Q521) that speaks of the works of healing that will take place when the Messiah makes his appearance, works that parallel closely Jesus' summary in his reply to the imprisoned and discouraged John the Baptist (Matt. 11:2–6; Luke 7:18–23). From this important discovery, scholars are now more open to affirm what the Gospels have said all along, that Jesus understood himself as Israel's Messiah. How to account for the ubiquity of the identity of Jesus as Messiah, had Jesus never thought of himself in these terms, was a question that apparently had not sufficiently impressed itself upon these skeptical scholars.

The important point in this event is that immediately after the woman's anointing of Jesus, Judas Iscariot departs to betray his master (Mark 14:10–11). The contrast between the named disciple, who commits an act of treachery, and the unnamed woman, who commits an act of devotion, has been commented upon frequently. It is a piece of literary artistry, to be sure. But sometimes overlooked is that this woman's actions very likely would have been reported to the ruling priests, with whom Judas struck his bargain. Not only would Judas earn his pay by directing the officers and thugs of the ruling priests to the place of Jesus' private prayer, he would have offered them testimony as to what Jesus taught and how his followers regarded him. The woman's anointing of Jesus would have been too important to miss. It would have provided all the more reason to destroy Jesus.

In the end, the Jewish authorities sought to kill Jesus not because he was a good man but because Jesus was perceived as a very serious political threat. His message of God's rule threatened the status quo, which the ruling priests did not want overturned. Jesus entered Jerusalem as the anointed son of David, he assumed authority in the temple precincts as though possessed of messianic authority, he appealed to the purpose of the temple in a way that recalled Solomon's dedication of the temple and in a way that implied him to be king, and he was in fact anointed by at least one follower, an anointing that in all probability was interpreted as having messianic significance. It is hardly surprising that an angry high priest would directly ask Jesus, "Are you the Messiah, the Son of God?" and that the Roman governor would place near the cross a placard that read, "This is Jesus, king of the Jews."

DID JESUS ANTICIPATE HIS DEATH?

Before considering the trial and execution of Jesus, we must ask if Jesus anticipated his death. Some critics insist that he did not: that it took him by surprise or that he had simply got caught up in a riot and was arrested along with others. I find this quite unlikely as a historical reading of the Gospels, for several reasons.

The obvious place to begin is with Jesus' formal predictions of his suffering and death (e.g., Mark 8:31; 9:31; 10:32–34, among others). Of course, many critical scholars claim that these passion predictions are prophecies after the fact, or what are sometimes called *vaticinia ex eventu* (prophecies from the event). It must be admitted that these predictions have a formulaic appearance and contain details (such as being mocked, spat upon, and scourged) that suggest knowledge of what in the end actually happened to Jesus. But even if it is acknowledged that the passion predictions have been edited or further stylized in the light of what actually happened to Jesus, it does not necessarily mean that he in fact did not anticipate his death, even death specifically by crucifixion. What is the evidence outside the formal passion predictions that would suggest that Jesus really did anticipate suffering and death?

First, I think it is probable that Jesus anticipated his death, for the violent fate of John the Baptist surely had impressed itself on him (Matt. 11:2–15; Mark 6:14–29; 9:13). It would be strange to think that it never occurred to Jesus that what had happened to his ally John might happen to him. In fact, Jesus may well have drawn this comparison and conclusion himself and spoke of it. In a saying whose wording and context admittedly are not easy to interpret, Jesus speaks of John the Baptist as Elijah, who "has come" but was not treated with respect. By analogy, Jesus, who already has directly linked his own ministry with John's, suggests the same fate also awaits him. He too will "go through many sufferings and be treated with contempt" (Mark

9:11–13). Accordingly, the execution of John surely suggested to Jesus that the same may well overtake him.

Second, and what I think is impressive evidence that Jesus anticipated his death, is the scene in Gethsemane. Here we see the frightened Jesus fall on his face, begging God to take away the cup of suffering (Mark 14:33–36). This is not the stuff of pious fiction or dogma. Indeed, it stands in stark contrast to the serene Jesus portrayed in John 17, where he communes with God in peace, prays for his disciples, and adds a prayer for all those who will follow after him.

What makes the Gethsemane scene compelling evidence is that Jesus' words and frightened behavior stand in tension with his earlier teaching, in which he exhorts his disciples to "take up their cross" and follow him (Mark 8:34). In view of such a teaching, it is hard to see how a story such as the Gethsemane prayer could circulate and find its way into the Gospel tradition if it were not based on solid, credible eyewitness testimony. It would simply be too risky for Jesus' identity if it were not true.

Third, if Jesus anticipated his death, we should expect that he attempted to find meaning in it during his life. In fact, that is the case. The widely attested "words of institution" (Mark 14:22–25; 1 Cor. 11:23–25; *Didache* 9:1–5) provide further evidence that Jesus anticipated his death and sought to understand it. His words allude to several important scriptures (Exod. 24:8; Jer. 31:31; Zech. 9:11). In the shedding of his blood, Jesus finds guarantee of the covenant and the kingdom of God. Luke's addition of "new," as in "the new covenant" (Luke 22:20), may well reflect Christian editing for clarification, but in all probability it correctly captures the sense of Jesus' words. The "new covenant" hearkens back to the promise of the prophet long ago: "The days are surely coming, says the LORD, when I will make a new covenant with the house of Israel and the house of Judah" (Jer. 31:31). The new covenant cannot be established until the blood of God's Son, Israel's Messiah, is shed.

The idea of the saving benefit of a righteous man's death is hardly unusual in the Jewish world, or in the Mediterranean world in general, for that matter. There are several expressions of the belief that the death of the righteous will benefit, or even save, God's people (e.g., 1 Macc 6:44; 4 Macc 1:11; 17:21–22; 18:3–4; *T. Moses* 9–10; Ps.-Philo, *Bib. Ant.* 18:5). Among the most important are traditions associated with the torture and death of the Maccabean martyrs, who in the second century BC bravely opposed the Syrian tyrant Antiochus IV: "And if our living Lord is angry for a little while, to rebuke and discipline us, he will again be reconciled with his own servants. . . . I, like my brothers, give up body and life for the laws of our ancestors, appealing to God to show mercy soon to our nation . . . and *through me and my brothers* to bring to an end the wrath of the Almighty that has justly fallen on our whole nation" (2 Macc 7:33, 37–38, NRSV, with emphasis added). Similarly, Jesus believed that God was angry with his people for having rejected his message. We see this in Jesus' weeping over the city (Luke 19:41–44; Matt. 23:37–39 = Luke 13:34–35) and in his ominous allusion to the shepherd in Zechariah 13:7, whom God would strike down.

If Jesus did anticipate his death, then one might also ask, did he anticipate his resurrection as well? Had he not anticipated being raised after death, it would have been very strange, for many pious Jews very much believed in the resurrection (Dan. 12:1–3; *1 Enoch* 22–27; 92–105; *Jub.* 23:11–31; 4 Macc 7:3; 4 Ezra 7:26–42; *2 Bar.* 21:23; 30:2–5; Josephus, *J.W.* 2.154, 165–66; *Ant.* 18.14, 16, 18).

One is reminded of the seven martyred sons and their mother, several of whom expressed their firmest conviction of the resurrection (2 Macc 7:14, 23, 29; cf. 4 Macc 8–17). Would Jesus have faced death and then, having earlier affirmed his belief in the resurrection (Mark 12:18–27), have expressed no faith in his own vindication? Surely not. It seems probable that Jesus would have reassured his disciples (and himself) with a confident prediction of his resurrection.

The words of Jesus, "after three days rise again" (Mark 8:31), and—in the other Gospels—"on the third day" (Matt. 16:21; Luke 9:22; cf. 1 Cor. 15:4), probably allude to the oracle of Hosea that promised the renewal of Israel:

> "After two days he will revive us;
>   on the third day he will raise us up,
>   that we may live before him." (6:2)

This is refracted, though, through the Aramaic tradition: "He will revive us *in the days of consolations that will come; on the day of the resurrection of the dead* he will raise us up and we shall live before him" (Hos. 6:2, according to the Targum, with italicized portion indicating differences in the Aramaic). Not only has the text been paraphrased to give expression to the resurrection (which was not exactly the original meaning of the underlying Hebrew), it has also taken on a messianic nuance with the words "in the days of consolations" (cf. 2 Sam. 23:1 in the Aramaic). The coherence of Jesus' words with the Aramaic tradition is striking.

Jesus' confidence that God would raise him up provides additional evidence that Jesus did in fact anticipate his death. More will be said about the resurrection of Jesus in chapter 3 below.

THE TRIAL OF JESUS

Since the nineteenth century the trial of Jesus has been hotly debated, often with reference to Christian anti-Semitism. Some scholars have argued that the trial of Jesus was entirely a Roman affair, while others have asserted that it was mostly a Jewish affair. Today most scholars rightly recognize the involvement both of Jewish and Roman authorities.

All four New Testament Gospels relate appearances of Jesus before Jewish and Roman authorities, who to one degree or another work in concert. According to Mark, Jesus is arrested by people acting under the authority of the ruling priests, scribes, and elders (14:43–50). Jesus is taken to the high priest (14:53). Jewish authorities then gather at "the courtyard of the high priest" (14:54), which may imply that the proceedings took place at the home of Caiaphas, though that is only an inference. The ruling priests and council seek testimony against Jesus (14:55–56). Various accusations are made, including Jesus' threat against the temple (14:57–58; cf. 13:1–2). When Jesus confesses that he is indeed the Messiah, the Son of God, who will be seated at the right hand, he is accused of blasphemy and condemned as deserving death (14:61–64). The following morning the Jewish authorities deliver Jesus to Pilate, the Roman prefect of Judea and Samaria (15:1). Pilate questions Jesus ("Are you the King of the Jews?") and offers to release him, as part of the governor's traditional "Passover pardon" (15:2–14). The crowd requests the release of Barabbas and calls for Jesus' death, whereupon Pilate gives Jesus up to be crucified (15:15).

There are distinctive elements in the other Gospels that further flesh out these events. The noticeable addition in Matthew is seen in the reference to the disturbing dream

Pilate's wife had, warning the governor to "have nothing to do with that innocent man" (27:19). The Matthean version of the trial before Pilate ends with the governor washing his hands and declaring that he is "innocent of this man's blood" (27:24), to which the crowd responds with the fateful words, "His blood be on us and on our children!" (27:25). Luke's version of the trial before Pilate exhibits a few more distinctive features. Jesus is accused of forbidding the payment of tribute or taxes to Caesar (23:2) and of stirring up the people (23:5). The evangelist also adds the interesting account of Herod Antipas meeting Jesus and of Pilate and Herod's newfound friendship (23:6–12). Luke also strongly emphasizes the innocence of Jesus (23:20–25). The innocent Jesus stands in stark contrast to the murderer Barabbas, whose release the crowd demands.

The trial of Jesus, especially before Pilate, is quite distinctive in the fourth Gospel. When arrested, Jesus is taken to Annas, a former high priest and father-in-law of Caiaphas, the current high priest (18:12–13). While being questioned, Jesus is struck (18:22–23). Thereafter Jesus is sent to Caiaphas (18:24) and from there to the Roman Praetorium (18:28). Here the fourth Gospel differs noticeably from the Synoptic Gospels, in that nothing is said of any interrogation or exchange between Caiaphas and Jesus. But the most distinctive feature of the trial of Jesus in the Gospel of John is the dialogue between Pilate and Jesus (18:29–38), in which Jesus declares that his kingdom "is not from this world" (18:36) and Pilate asks, "What is truth?" (18:38). From a theological point of view, perhaps the most important feature is the emphasis on the legal point that the Jewish authorities were not allowed to execute anyone (18:31–32). Not only would this guarantee crucifixion (and, therefore, Jesus would be "lifted up"; cf.

12:32), but it may have served an apologetic purpose, mitigating the embarrassment of execution at the hands of the Roman authorities.

The trial of Jesus is mentioned in passing elsewhere in the New Testament writings. In the Pentecost sermon, Peter refers to Jesus as "a man attested to you by God with deeds of power, wonders, and signs that God did through him among you . . . handed over to you according to the definite plan and foreknowledge of God, you crucified and killed by the hands of those outside the law" (Acts 2:22–23). Peter's "you" refers to the Jewish people (cf. Acts 2:14), while the "lawless men" doubtlessly refers to the Roman authorities. The point is made again in the temple sermon, where Peter this time accuses fellow Jews: "God . . . has glorified his servant Jesus, whom you handed over and rejected in the presence of Pilate . . . and you killed the Author of life" (Acts 3:13–15). Peter's accusations presuppose (rightly) the collaboration between Jewish and Roman authorities in examining and condemning Jesus. We hear this again in Acts as part of an interpretation of Psalm 2, which asks why the nations plot against the Lord and his Anointed. The apostles in prayer declare that "For in this city, in fact, both Herod and Pontius Pilate, with the Gentiles and the peoples of Israel, gathered together against your holy servant Jesus, whom you anointed" (Acts 4:27). This theme is echoed in a sermon attributed to Paul: "Even though they found no cause for a sentence of death, they asked Pilate to have him killed" (Acts 13:27). Also, in one of the Pastoral Letters the author charges his readers, "in the presence of God, who gives life to all things, and of Christ Jesus, who in his testimony before Pontius Pilate made the good confession" (1 Tim. 6:13).

According to the Gospels Jesus was arrested at night, more or less in private, while in prayer at a place called Gethsemane on the Mount of Olives. Mark describes the arresting group as "a crowd with swords and clubs, from the chief priests, the scribes, and the elders" (14:43; cf. John 18:3: "a detachment of soldiers together with police from the chief priests and the Pharisees"). This group knew where to find Jesus because of information received from Judas Iscariot and because he himself led them to Jesus (Mark 14:10–11, 43–45). Both of these details—men sent by the ruling priests armed with weapons and priests offering bribes—are in a general sense corroborated by Josephus, who tells of similar actions taken by the most powerful of the ruling priests in the first century (cf. Josephus, *Ant.* 20.205–7 ["servants who were utter rascals"], 213 ["using his wealth . . . bribes"]; *t. Menah.* 13.18–19, 21 ["their servants come and beat us with clubs"]).

Exactly where Jesus was taken the evening of his arrest is not clear. Mark says he was taken to the high priest (14:53; followed by Luke 22:54), but this priest is not named. Matthew identifies him as Caiaphas (26:57). The fourth evangelist complicates things by saying that "first they took him to Annas, who was the father-in-law of Caiaphas" (John 18:13a). Annas is called "high priest" (18:19), even though it was his son-in-law who was actually in office "that year," that is, the year of Jesus' execution (18:13b). According to the fourth Gospel, Annas interrogates Jesus and then sends him to Caiaphas (18:24). Either the Synoptics did not know of this visit to Annas, or they chose to omit it.

The ensuing examination of Jesus before the Jewish authorities focused on two points: the allegation of a threat against the temple and the identity of Jesus. First, the testimony of the witnesses who said, "We heard him say, 'I will destroy this temple that is made with hands, and in three days I will build another, not made with hands'" (Mark 14:58), alludes to Jesus' prophecy of coming judgment on Jerusalem and her temple. He implies as much in his temple action (Mark 11:17) and in his vineyard parable (12:1–12), and he asserts it in his prophecy (13:1–2). Accordingly, the testimony of these witnesses was not entirely false; Jesus said something to this effect (see also John 2:19). What makes it false, though, is that Jesus warned of judgment *at God's hands, not at his*. Jesus had no plans to destroy and rebuild Jerusalem's temple. But he warned that God would destroy it if his people, especially the ruling priesthood, did not repent.

What brings the hearing before the Jewish council to a dramatic conclusion is Jesus' confession. The high priest asked him: "Are you the Messiah, the Son of the Blessed One?" (Mark 14:61). As we have seen, he has every reason to ask this question. Jesus' entry into the city, the shouts of the crowd, his audacious behavior in the temple precincts, and the report of his anointing all point to a messianic self-understanding. Even his ministry of healing and exorcism could be understood as paralleling the remarkable stories about the famous King Solomon. To the high priest's question Jesus replies boldly:

"I am; and
'you will see the Son of man
seated at the right hand of the Power,'
and 'coming with the clouds of heaven.'" (14:62)

Jesus' reply combines two Old Testament passages, both concerned with judgment. The words "Son of man" and "coming with the clouds of heaven" are taken from Daniel 7:13, while the words "seated at the right hand" are drawn from Psalm 110:1. Both Daniel 7 and Psalm 110 envision scenes in which God's enemies will be judged. Though our contemporary ears may not rightly hear the audacity of Jesus' claim, the high priest clearly does, and he condemns Jesus for it, not only for his daring claim to be God's anointed Son, but for implying that he will sit in judgment on the high priest, as though he were an enemy of God. It is hardly surprising that Jesus' bold reply is met with shouts of blasphemy and calls for death (14:63–65).

That morning the Jewish authorities confer and decide to send Jesus to Pilate, the Roman governor. The ball is now in Pilate's court. The Jewish rulers have decided. From this point on all they can do is cheer or jeer from the sidelines. But before we turn to Jesus' trial before Pilate, one thing needs to be made crystal clear: the Jewish people should never be blamed for the condemnation and death of Jesus. Not only is such an accusation bad theology, it is bad history. Historically speaking, Jesus was condemned by a very small number of influential Jewish men. He was not condemned by the people as a whole. Even those who cried out for his crucifixion later in the day were but a relatively small number. Theologically speaking, Jesus died for the sins of the whole human race. In that sense we all sent him to the cross. No one particular people should be blamed. Now on to Pilate.

According to all four Gospels the focus of Pilate's examination of Jesus was on the allegation that Jesus had presented himself as the king of the Jews (Mark 15:2; Matt.

27:11; Luke 23:3; John 18:33). This appears to be confirmed by Jesus' crucifixion as "King of the Jews" (Mark 15:18, 26, with parallels in the other Gospels). It has been persuasively argued that such an epithet was no Christian creation, confessional or otherwise. Christians regarded Jesus as the Messiah (or Christ), Son of God, Lord, and Savior, not "King of the Jews," a title the Roman Senate granted to Herod the Great (cf. Josephus, *J.W.* 1.282; *Ant.* 14.36; 15.373, 409; 16.291).

Under normal circumstances, I doubt that Pilate would have much hesitation in executing a troublemaker. But the occasion is the eve of Passover, the holiest of the Jewish holidays. Worse yet, Passover celebrated God's deliverance of his people from foreign bondage. Pilate would certainly have made this connection in knowing the workings of the people over whom he ruled. Though he did not lack in desire to demonstrate his and Rome's power, sustaining his position as governor of this region and keeping the *pax romana* (Roman peace) at times required greater precision and acumen. Did he really want to put to death a popular prophet and healer on the eve of the Passover, just outside the walls of Jerusalem? Perhaps a beating or imprisonment would suffice. Let the people decide.

THE OFFER OF A PASSOVER PARDON

All four New Testament Gospels know of Pilate's so-called Passover pardon (Mark 15:6–15; Matt. 27:15–23; Luke 23:18–25; John 19:10–12). Although some critical scholars have cast doubts on the historicity of this tradition, it is improbable that inauthentic tradition, whose falsity could so readily be exposed, would be utilized by all four evangelists.

Besides, there are other accounts of Roman and other officials releasing prisoners on occasion of special days that are not questioned. For example, the Roman historian Livy (c. 25 BC) speaks of special cases where prisoners were released ("Books from the Foundation of the City," 5.13.8). Herod's son Archelaus, as the newly appointed ethnarch of Judea and Samaria (4 BC), acquiesced to popular demands to release many prisoners (Josephus, *Ant.* 17.204). Josephus also says that Albinus, procurator of the whole of Herod's former kingdom (AD 62–64), released many prisoners as he prepared to leave office, something akin to a last-minute presidential pardon. One official document, dating from the year AD 85, reads, "You were worthy of scourging . . . but I give you to the crowds" (*P.Florence* 61). Here a Roman official forgoes scourging, which was often a prelude to crucifixion, and releases the criminal. In a slightly different scenario, Pliny the Younger, governor of Bithynia (in Asia Minor) in the days of Emperor Trajan (c. AD 110), refers to pardons for criminals, whereby "these people were released upon their petition to the proconsuls, or their lieutenants" (*Epistles* 10.31). Finally, according to the Mishna (c. AD 200), the edited and published collection of Jewish oral law, it is said that "they may slaughter (the Passover lamb) for one . . . whom they have promised to bring out of prison" on the Passover (*m. Pesahim* 8:6).

The evidence as a whole suggests that Roman rulers, as well as at least one Herodian prince, on occasion released prisoners (so apparently did other rulers in the eastern Mediterranean). This was done for purely political reasons, to satisfy the demands of the crowds and to curry their favor. The Passover pardon, therefore, reflected Pilate's shrewd political instincts, not political weakness or human kindness. The Passover pardon was intended to

show Roman respect for the great Jewish holiday, in effect
to say, "In keeping with your celebration of freedom from
bondage we shall set free anyone of your choosing." The
tradition of the Passover pardon gave Pilate the opportunity to pass responsibility for the fate of Jesus onto the
shoulders of his accusers. If they so badly want him dead,
then let them take responsibility for passing judgment.
Pilate is neither cowardly nor principled. He is clever.

Another factor that supports the historicity of the
Passover pardon is the improbability of asserting such a
custom, if there had been none. If Pilate had not released
prisoners on the Passover or on other holidays, or at least
on one occasion, the evangelists' claim that he did so could
have quickly and easily been shown to be false and would
therefore have occasioned embarrassment for or even dis-
credited altogether the early church. That all three of the
later evangelists take over the story (and the fourth evangelist probably did so independently of the Synoptic Gospels)
argues that no such embarrassment clung to the story.

Knowing, then, that Jesus had been handed over to
him on account of envy, Pilate treads carefully. Before condemning Jesus to death, he seeks in essence a plebiscite, a
decree from the people. Did the people really want Jesus
executed, or was it only the few ruling priests who brought
the charges and demanded his death? There is no interest
in justice here; only politics are at work. Pilate probably
knew that Jesus was popular. He was not about to risk
offending the populace, especially at Passover season, and
so instigate a riot. This was the very thing he wished to
avoid. Some might challenge this interpretation by pointing
to incidents in which Pilate seemed more than willing to
use violence against his subjects. But in these cases, Pilate

was defending his own actions. In the case of Jesus, Pilate has nothing at stake other than maintaining the peace.

As the scene unfolds, the ruling priests urge the crowd to call for the release of Jesus bar Abba—not Jesus of Nazareth (Mark 15:11–15). They have vigorously lobbied the governor. Now they vigorously lobby the crowd. From their point of view, the danger that Jesus of Nazareth would be released was a very real one. After all, Jesus was known as a popular teacher and healer, and led no army. He was therefore not an obvious threat to Rome. At most, he was guilty of speaking of a coming kingdom of God and of having a key role in it—things not too different from visions and dreams of others. Perhaps it was politically more expedient to release him than make a martyr of him. Hence, the ruling priests encouraged the crowd to call for the release of bar Abba, or Barabbas (on noisy crowds clamoring before a Roman authority, see Acts 24:1; Josephus, *Ant.* 18.264–73).

If Jesus of Nazareth is not to be released, then what shall the governor do with him? The alternatives are fairly obvious: either execution or imprisonment. But Pilate forces the crowd to make the decision. This way, he can "wash his hands" (literally in Matt. 27:24) of the matter. Politically, Pilate has acted shrewdly and entirely in keeping with his character as we know it from unsympathetic sources (e.g., Philo and Josephus).

Once again "they"—that is, the crowd (cf. Mark 15:11)—as well as the ruling priests themselves, shout their demands to Pilate. They shout for the release of Barabbas, but in reference to Jesus, they shout "Crucify him!" They do not want prison for Jesus; they want the ultimate penalty for him: crucifixion. The death of Jesus will hopefully end his movement and fatally discourage his closest followers.

In asking, "Why, what evil has he done?" (Mark 15:14), Pilate has committed no "tactical blunder," as one commentator suggests, nor is his answer "feeble," as another has supposed. The governor is happy to accommodate the ruling priests' recommendation that Jesus be put to death— as long as in doing so he incurs no political risks. His only concern is that his condemnation of Jesus not provoke the Jewish people or be seen as yet another example of Roman brutality. Pilate is not about to create a problem for himself. He wishes only to extricate himself from responsibility (as also does the Roman proconsul Gallio in Corinth, who judges the controversy set before him as a Jewish dispute and not one that falls under his jurisdiction; cf. Acts 18:12–17). If the crowd insists that Jesus be crucified, he would like to know why and he would like for them to announce it publicly.

Not wishing to provoke the crowd, Pilate ultimately releases Barabbas (Mark 15:15). Again, this maneuver is not one that shows weakness. Indeed, in this case, Pilate wishes not to offend his *allies*, the ruling priests. In his other controversies, the Roman governor came into conflict with the "rabble" or commoners, not the ruling priests. What he has done here is to accede to the wishes of the ruling priests, but not until he is satisfied that to do so was not a mistake. Having released Barabbas to the people, Pilate hands Jesus over to the Roman troops, who will carry out the crucifixion.

The Gospels' portrait of Pilate as wavering, wishing to release Jesus, but finally acquiescing to the demands of Jerusalem's influential elite has often been questioned. Many assume that this portrait grew out of apologetic interests, in a desire to present Jesus and early Christianity on the side of Rome. It was the Jewish leaders, after all, not the Roman governor, who desired Jesus' death; so goes the argument. That the evangelists literarily exploited the story of the wavering, uncertain Pilate is quite probable, but its wholesale invention is quite doubtful. When we remember the political and social setting of Jewish Palestine in the time of Pilate, we should not be surprised that Pilate was reluctant to execute in such a public and provocative manner a popular prophet from Galilee, whose many followers were present in Jerusalem. Nailing Jesus to a cross could very well instigate a riot, the very thing Pilate hoped to avoid. If Jesus had no military intentions, then he was little more than a pest. A beating and some jail time would suffice. But no, the ruling priests wanted him dead. Pilate obliged, but only when it had been made clear that the decision to have Jesus executed was not really his.

THE MOCKERY OF JESUS

Crucifixion victims were often mocked before and during execution. In the case of Jesus, his mockery began with the Jewish council. His face is covered and he is ordered to "prophesy" (Mark 14:65). After all, if he were truly a prophet, he would possess clairvoyance and, without benefit of sight, could identify those who struck him. I am sure the officers and thugs employed by the ruling priests found it all quite amusing.

The soldiers under the command of Governor Pilate also mocked Jesus, this time reflecting the Roman fashion: "And they clothed him in a purple cloak; and after twisting some thorns into a crown, they put it on him. And they began saluting him, 'Hail, King of the Jews!' They struck his head with a reed, spat upon him, and knelt down in homage to him" (Mark 15:17–19). The mockery of the soldiers is modeled after the homage paid to Caesar. The crown of thorns, meant to resemble a wreath of laurel worn by Caesar, is part of the mockery of Jesus. This mockery includes a purple cloak, a reed (symbolizing the scepter), and being addressed as a king (Mark 15:18–19). The offer of spiced vinegar to the dying Jesus is also probably part of the ongoing mockery (Mark 15:23; Luke 23:36), in that this drink mimics spiced wine, often served to kings. Sources from late antiquity describe others mocked in a similar fashion.

The mockery of Jesus as a Jewish king finds an approximate parallel in Philo, an older contemporary. It was on the occasion of King Agrippa's visit to Alexandria, where the people seized a lunatic named Carabas, a street person who was often made sport of (*In Flaccum* 36–39). They

> drove the poor fellow into the gymnasium and set him up high to be seen by all and put on his head a sheet of byblus spread out wide for a diadem, clothed the rest of his body with a rug for a royal robe, while someone who had noticed a piece of the native papyrus thrown away in the road gave it to him for his scepter. And when as in some theatrical farce he had received the insignia of kingship and had been tricked out as a king, young men carrying rods on their shoulders as spearmen stood on either side of him in imitation of a bodyguard. Then others approached him, some pretending to salute him, others to sue for justice, others to consult him on state affairs. Then from the multitudes there rang out a tremendous shout hailing him as *Mari* [Aramaic: "My lord"], which is said to be the name for "lord" with the Syrians.

The mockery of Agrippa I is quite significant, well illustrating the mockery to which Jesus was subjected. It does not, however, require us to conclude that Mark and the other evangelists are dependent in some way on this incident or on Philo's work itself. Other incidents approximate the mockery of Jesus. One thinks of the harsh and humiliating treatment of deposed Emperor Vitellius (AD 69) at the hands of Roman soldiers, who mockingly made the former emperor revisit various stations where at one time he was held in honor (cf. Dio Cassius 64.20–21). Now the honor has turned to shame and mockery.

The mockery of Jesus also mimics aspects of the Roman triumph, whereby Caesar is hailed as emperor and receives homage. The purple cloak, the crown of thorns (resembling the crown of ivy), the reed with which Jesus is struck on the head, and the bowing in mock homage are all components of the apparel worn and homage received by the Roman emperor, who at the triumph wore a purple robe and laurel wreath and held a scepter (e.g., Dio Cassius 6.23; 44.11 [Julius Caesar]; Appian, *Civil Wars* 5.130 [Augustus]; Dio Cassius 59.25.3 [Gaius Caligula]). Being dressed in purple would also recall the attire of Hellenistic kings of an earlier period (cf. 1 Macc 10:20 ["purple robe and golden crown"], 62 ["clothe him in purple"]; 11:58 ["to dress in purple"]; 14:43–44 ["clothed in purple"]; Luke 16:19 ["dressed in purple"]).

We think too of the savage and humiliating treatment of Maccabean martyr Eleazar, who was stripped, scourged, tortured, and then in his dying breath prayed for the salvation of Israel (4 Macc 6:1–30). One is also reminded of the deposition recording the words of the new emperor Hadrian and a Jewish embassy, with reference to the Jewish revolt that occurred toward the end of Trajan's reign (AD 115–17). In this fragmentary document mention is made of the mockery of a would-be monarch: "Paulus (spoke) about the king, how they brought him forth and (mocked him); and Theon read the edict of Lupus ordering them to lead him forth for Lupus to make fun of the king . . ." (*P.Louvre* 68 1.1–7). Writing in the early second century AD, Plutarch (*Pompey* 24.7–8) relates a story in which pirates mocked a prisoner who had claimed the rights of Roman citizenship. They dressed him up ("threw a toga on him"), extended to him various honors (including falling to their knees), then finally made him walk the plank.

Everything we are told about Jesus' arrest, trial(s), and mockery is consistent with what we know of Roman practice in the first century and consistent with the political and social establishment of Judea in the time of Jesus. Although hyper-critics have called into question this and that detail, there is every reason to regard the Gospel accounts of the juridical process that overtook Jesus of Nazareth as essentially reliable. Most of the noted objections, then, amount to something other than valid historical reasoning.

THE CRUCIFIXION OF JESUS

Jesus was put to death by crucifixion, a form of execution practiced in late antiquity, whereby a person was tied or nailed to a pole or cross. To be crucified is, literally, to be "staked." Crucifixion was practiced in the eastern Mediterranean long before the Romans adopted the practice. It was practiced by Persians (cf. Herodotus 1.128.2; 3.125.3) and other peoples, such as Assyrians, Scythians, and Thracians. Alexander the Great is said to have crucified thousands (cf. Curtius Rufus, *Hist. Alex.* 4.4.17), and his successors continued the practice. It is not surprising, then, that in time the Romans adopted this form of execution. It was primarily reserved for murderous or rebellious slaves (and for this reason was known as "slaves' punishment"; Latin: *servile supplicium*). Its primary purpose was to deter rebellion.

Some readers may not be aware that Jewish authorities before the Roman period also practiced crucifixion. Most notorious was Alexander Jannaeus (ruled 102–76 BC), who, Josephus tells us, on one occasion crucified a large number of Pharisees who had opposed him and had allied themselves to a foreign enemy (*J.W.* 1.97–98; cf. *Ant.* 13.380). Josephus's testimony helps explain a reference in the Dead Sea Scrolls, where in one of the *pesharim* (a type of scriptural interpretation common in these scrolls from Qumran) there is reference to the "Lion of Wrath" (understood to be Alexander Jannaeus) who "used to hang men alive" (4Q169 frags. 3–4, col. I, line 7). This may well be in reference to the incident mentioned by Josephus. Indeed, the practice of crucifixion in Israel in late antiquity, whether by Jewish authorities or Roman authorities, influenced the understanding of Deuteronomy 21:22–23: "When someone is convicted of a crime punishable by death and is executed, and you hang him on a tree, his corpse must not remain all night upon the tree; you shall bury him that same day, for anyone hung on a tree is under God's curse. You must not defile the land that the LORD your God is giving you for possession." Originally, the passage meant that the body of the executed man was to be hung on the tree, then taken down and buried before nightfall. But by the time of Jesus, the passage was understood to apply also to those hung while still alive, a practical alteration that reflects the common practice of crucifixion.

As a prelude to his crucifixion, Jesus is scourged (Mark 15:15). Scourging was apparently standard precrucifixion procedure in Roman times (cf. *Digesta* 48.19.8.3;

Josephus, *J.W.* 2.306). It was done with a whip made of
several leather straps, to which were attached sharp, abra-
sive items, such as nails, glass, or rocks. Scourging resulted
in severe laceration of the skin and damage to the flesh
beneath. Jesus son of Ananias should be mentioned again.
His prophecies of Jerusalem's doom resulted in his being
brought before the Roman governor. Although in the end
the man was not executed (as the ruling priests wished), he
was "flayed to the bone with scourges" (*J.W.* 6.304), the
same word used in reference to Jesus of Nazareth. Indeed,
Jesus himself warned his followers that they too face the
danger of scourging (cf. Matt. 10:17; 23:34).

Supporting the weakened state that Jesus would have
been in (most immediately from the scourging), Mark 15:21
relates that the Romans "compelled a passer-by, who was
coming in from the country, to carry his cross; it was Simon
of Cyrene, the father of Alexander and Rufus." The authen-
ticity of this scene is supported by the observation that Jesus
had earlier instructed his disciples to be ready and willing to
take up the cross and come after him (Mark 8:34). It is not
likely that early Christians would invent a story about Jesus
being unable to follow his own instruction to the letter.

Mark's reference to the names of Simon's sons,
Alexander and Rufus, may suggest that these men were
known to Mark's church. What we have here in Mark's narrative may well be eyewitness testimony, in which it was
remembered that Jesus was beaten so severely he could not
carry his cross, even though in earlier and happier times he
had exhorted his own followers to be prepared to do so.
Perhaps Simon and eventually his sons also became followers of the man whose cross Simon carried.

Jesus eventually arrives at the place of execution and
he is crucified. The Gospels say that a *titulus*, or placard,

was placed on the cross of Jesus (cf. John 19:19; Matt. 27:37; Mark 15:26; Luke 23:38) and that it was written in more than one language, describing Jesus as "King of the Jews." The epithet "King of the Jews" is Roman and was originally applied to Herod the Great (cf. Josephus, *Ant.* 15.409: "the king of the Jews, Herod"). As mentioned already, this epithet did not originate in Christian circles, for Christians referred to Jesus with different titles. The significance of the *titulus* is that it confirms the messianic self-understanding of Jesus. Jesus had encouraged his disciples to regard him as Israel's anointed king, or, in the language of Rome, the "King of the Jews."

As a matter of custom, Roman authorities placed crosses along well-traveled highways, on tops of hills, and at city gates. The condemned man usually carried the crossbeam, or *patibulum* (cf. Plautus, *Carbonaria* 2; *Miles gloriosus* 2.4.6–7 §359–360; Plutarch, *Mor.* 554A—B), sometimes with a *titulus* around his neck, declaring his name and punishment, later to be affixed to the upright cross (cf. Suetonius, *Caligula* 32.2; Dio Cassius 54.3.6–7). This cruel punishment later also befell Christians. Fourth-century church historian and apologist Eusebius tells of one Attalus the Christian, who "was led around the amphitheatre and a placard was carried before him on which was written in Latin, 'This is Attalus, the Christian'" (*Hist. Eccl.* 5.1.44).

Normally crucifixion victims were left to die, however long that took (sometimes several days). The longer delay of death for victims of crucifixion is evident in that on occasion friends and relatives were allowed to feed their loved one (cf. Matt. 27:34; Mark 15:23; John 19:28–29). It was typical protocol for guards to be stationed by the cross until the victim expired, in part due to possible attempts by friends or relatives to rescue the victim. The bodies of the crucified were usually left unburied, to rot and to be picked apart by birds and animals (though Roman law did permit bodies to be taken down and buried; cf. *Digesta* 48.24.1, 3; Josephus, *Life* 420–21). I will leave the questions and issues surrounding the burial of Jesus until chapter 2, which is devoted solely to that subject.

According to Cicero (*Verr.* 2.5.168) and Josephus (*J.W.* 7.203), crucifixion was the worst form of death (see also the disturbing comments in Juvenal, *Satires* 14.77–78; Suetonius, *Augustus* 13.1–2; Horace, *Epistles* 1.16.48; Seneca, *Dialogue* 3.2.2; 6.20.3; Isidore of Seville, *Etymologia* 5.27.34; *Mek.* on Exod. 15:18 [*Shirata* §10]). Indeed, the words "cross" and "crucify" actually derive from the word for torture (Latin: *cruciare*). The primary political and social purpose of crucifixion was deterrence: "Whenever we crucify the condemned, the most crowded roads are chosen, where the most people can see and be moved by this terror. For penalties relate not so much to retribution as to their exemplary effect" (Ps.-Quintilian, *Declamations* 274; Aristophanes, *Thesmophoriazusae* 1029; Ps.-Manetho, *Apotelesmatica* 4.198–200; cf. Josephus, *J.W.* 5.450–51).

In the Gospels the soldiers who crucify Jesus divide his garments among themselves (Matt. 27:35; Mark 15:24; Luke 23:34; John 19:23–24). This is consistent with Roman practice (cf. *Digesta* 48.20.1). Tacitus, for example, tells us that "people sentenced to death forfeited their property" (*Annals* 6.29).

THE DEATH OF JESUS

The death of Jesus comes suddenly and dramatically. According to the Synoptic Gospels (Matt. 27:45; Mark

15:33; Luke 23:44), at about three in the afternoon Jesus suddenly cries out: *"Elo-i, Elo-i, lama sabach-thani?"* These Aramaic words, taken from Psalm 22:1, mean "My God, my God, why have you forsaken me?" Interpreters are perplexed. How are these words to be understood?

The details of Psalm 22 are echoed in various places in the passion narrative. Here, though, we have an explicit quotation, and one that is on the lips of Jesus. Some wonder if Jesus has the whole psalm in mind, especially the concluding part that relates vindication and restoration:

> I will tell of your name to my brothers and sisters;
>   in the midst of the congregation I will praise you . . .
> For he did not despise or abhor
>   the affliction of the afflicted;
> he did not hide his face from him,
>   but heard when he cried to him. . . .
> Posterity will serve him;
>   future generations will be told about the Lord,
> and proclaim his deliverance to a people yet unborn,
>   saying that he has done it. (vv. 22, 24, 30–31, NRSV,
>   modified according to the Hebrew)

Perhaps Jesus did have the whole of the psalm in mind, including the optimistic conclusion, but the reality of his sense of abandonment must not be minimized. Jesus has not lost his faith in God, as the twofold address, "My God, my God," might imply on its own. However, he clearly feels utterly abandoned. It is not surprising that the later evangelists choose different concluding utterances: "Father, into your hands I commend my spirit" (Luke 23:46); "It is finished" (John 19:30). The seemingly faith- and identity-denying words Jesus utters may well have been capitalized

on by some seeking to discredit him and even avoided by
those who followed after him. Again, except that they be historically true, these words are much too scandalous to report.

As he is staked to the cross, bystanders think Jesus
has called for Elijah (*eloi* ["my God"] approximating the
sound of *elia* ["Elijah"]). We are told that "someone ran,
filled a sponge with sour wine, put it on a stick, and gave it
to him to drink" (Mark 15:36). If this act was one of mockery, and not of sympathy, the soldiers probably would not
have hindered him. "Let us see whether Elijah will come to
take him down" may be part of the mockery and, if so, it
parallels what the ruling priests said earlier: "Let the
Messiah, the King of Israel, come down from the cross now,
so that we may see and believe" (Mark 15:32).

It is possible that a sympathetic bystander races up to
Jesus, to give him a stimulant to help keep Jesus conscious
long enough to see if Elijah would indeed appear, either in
his eschatological role (as Jesus, it would have been assumed,
hoped), or in his occasional role as assistant of the troubled
and stricken. It is more probable, however, that the gesture is
part of the mockery that has been going on since the conclusion of the hearing before the ruling priests (Mark 14:65).
While on the cross, Jesus has been mocked as the one who
threatened to destroy and rebuild the temple in three days
(15:29), he has been invited to come down from the cross
and so convince skeptics that he really is Israel's King
Messiah (15:32), and now the mockers wish to see "whether
Elijah will come" in answer to Jesus' anguished cry.

The bystanders do not have long to wait. "Then
Jesus gave a loud cry and breathed his last" (Mark 15:37).
The act of shouting is itself the death. That is, Jesus does
not shout out and then a moment later dies. His death man-

ifests itself *as a shout.* By telling it this way, the evangelist Mark, if not the tradition before him, shows that Jesus' very death displays his power; the release of his spirit (as implied in the verb *exepneusen*) is awesome.

Stunned by what he has witnessed, the centurion declares, "Truly this man was God's Son!" (Mark 15:39). Impressed by the manner of Jesus' death and the signs that attend it, the Roman centurion confesses of Jesus what he should only confess of the Roman emperor: Caesar is not the "son of God"; Jesus the crucified Messiah is. The mockery is now over. In calling Jesus the Son of God, the centurion has switched his allegiance from Caesar, the official "son of God," to Jesus, the real Son of God. The centurion now ascribes to Jesus what he had earlier ascribed to Caesar: Caesar is not *divi filius* ("son of God," alluding to the Latin title of the great emperor Augustus). Jesus is.

THE THEOLOGICAL IMPLICATIONS

The theological implications of the death of Jesus are several and varied. From the Jewish perspective that embraced aspects of the popular messianism in late antiquity, Jesus is a failed Messiah. The Messiah is supposed to prevail over Israel's enemies, as seen in several writings from this period. According to the men of Qumran, at least as we find in the War Scroll and related scrolls, the Messiah will lead his priestly warriors to victory over the hated Romans. Indeed, according to one scroll (4Q285, called the Rule of War), the Messiah, the Branch of David, will personally slay the Roman emperor. We find similar sentiments expressed in the *Psalms of Solomon* 17:

Lord, you chose David to be king over Israel,
    and swore to him about his descendants forever,
    that his kingdom should not fail before you.
Undergird him with the strength to destroy
      the unrighteous rulers,
    to purge Jerusalem from gentiles . . .
    to destroy the unlawful nations
      with the word of his mouth. . . .
He will gather a holy people whom he will lead
      in righteousness;
and he will judge the tribes of the people. . . .
He will not tolerate unrighteousness (even)
      to pause among them,
    and any person who knows wickedness
      shall not live with them. . . .
And he will purge Jerusalem (and make it) holy
      as it was even from the beginning.
                      (vv. 4, 22, 24, 26, 27, 30)

But Jesus gained no victory over the Romans. The Gentiles have not been driven out. His rule ended before it began. Instead of enthronement, his end was crucifixion; and as already has been mentioned, crucifixion was a degrading form of execution, reserved for slaves and the worst of the criminals.

A major reason for doubting the messianic identity of Jesus, on the part of the Jewish people, was the fact that Jesus died by crucifixion. This is the objection raised against Jesus in the Gospel of John: "We have heard from the law that the Messiah remains forever. How can you say that the Son of Man must be lifted up?" (John 12:34). This objection continued to be raised by Jewish writers. It is the very point raised by Trypho in Justin Martyr's second-century *Dialogue with Trypho the Jew*. Jesus may well have fulfilled prophecy; he may well have performed many impressive miracles; he may even have been raised from the dead; but where in Scripture does it say he was to be crucified and to die so shameful a death? In the end Trypho cannot bring himself to believe that Jesus of Nazareth, who suffered under Pontius Pilate, is Israel's Messiah and God's Son.

Of course, from the Roman perspective Jesus is little more than an executed criminal. There is no honor in such a death. Indeed, it is the death of slaves and the worst malefactors. Little wonder an ancient Christian song in honor of Christ has words that link Jesus with slaves:

taking the form of a slave . . .
he humbled himself
and became obedient to the point of death—
even death on a cross.   (Phil. 2:7–8)

But from Jesus' perspective, a perspective his disciples will embrace after the resurrection, his death has opened up a new understanding of sacrifice and atonement. The death of the one has atoned for the sin of the many. The promised new covenant has been established. The awaited redemption of Israel can now happen, but without a violent overthrow of Gentile powers. The Gentile nations will be conquered by the good news of the rule of God and of the atoning death of his Son, not by the sword.

But on the Friday afternoon in which Jesus died, none of this occurred to the disciples. Their master was dead. Their movement had been stopped in its tracks. They themselves had fled. Only Peter, a few women, and a few others lingered behind to see what would happen. Of

these only the women had courage enough to observe the
place where Jesus was buried.

FURTHER READING

Bammel, E., and C. F. D. Moule, eds. *Jesus and the Politics
of His Day*. Cambridge: Cambridge University
Press, 1984.

Brown, R. E. *The Death of the Messiah: From Gethsemane
to the Grave. A Commentary on the Passion Narratives in the Four Gospels*. 2 vols. Anchor Bible
Reference Library 7. New York: Doubleday, 1994.

Carrol, J. T., and J. B. Green, with R. E. Van Voorst,
J. Marcus, and D. Senior, *The Death of Jesus in Early
Christianity*. Peabody, MA: Hendrickson, 1995.

Chilton, B. "The Trial of Jesus Reconsidered." In *Jesus in
Context: Temple, Purity, and Restoration*. Edited by
B. Chilton and C. A. Evans, 481–500. Arbeiten zur
Geschichte des antiken Judentums und des
Urchristentums 39. Leiden: Brill, 1997.

Green, J. B. *The Death of Jesus*. Wissenschaftliche Unter-
suchungen zum Neuen Testament 2.33. Tübingen:
Mohr Siebeck, 1988.

Hengel, M. *Crucifixion*. London: SCM; Philadelphia:
Fortress, 1977.

McGing, B. C. "Pontius Pilate and the Sources." *Catholic
Biblical Quarterly* 53 (1991): 416–38.

Sherwin-White, A. N. *The Trial of Christ: Historicity and
Chronology in the Gospels*. London: SPCK, 1965.

Chapter Two

THE SILENCE OF BURIAL

Craig A. Evans

In recent years the reading public has been surprised and befuddled with some outlandish theories about Jesus' burial, and in some cases, nonburial. In a book published in the mid-1990s, a well-known New Testament scholar and frequent guest on news programs and documentaries made the startling claim that in all probability the body of Jesus was not buried at all, at least not in a tomb, as Christians for two thousand years have thought. This scholar suggested that Jesus' body was either left hanging on the cross, or at most was cast into a shallow ditch where it was eaten by dogs. This remarkable theory made headlines around the world. Why this idea has not the slightest chance of being correct is discussed below.

More recently, another writer, who pretends to do serious research but whose work utterly lacks respectability, has suggested that Jesus was indeed buried, but that he was comatose and later with the aid of friends and collaborators (among whom was Roman governor Pilate!) was rescued from the tomb. The "evidence" put forward for this hypothesis is quite bizarre and unconvincing. Fortunately, this piece of pseudo-scholarship received in the popular media the debunking it richly deserved.

More credible writers and commentators have from time to time raised doubts about the New Testament Gospels' accounts of the burial of Jesus, yet I find much of their skepticism a bit strange and running straight against the evidence of the New Testament. After all, we are told that three women observed where Jesus was buried and then returned to the tomb early Sunday morning (Mark 15:47; 16:1–4). They knew where Jesus had been buried and knew where to return for graveside mourning. One would think that fictional accounts of Jesus' burial would feature men as principal witnesses, not women, who in late antiquity were not always respected as credible. Additionally, the story of the tomb of Jesus receives important corroboration in Paul, who speaks of the burial of Jesus (1 Cor. 15:3–4). When Paul says Jesus "was buried," a tomb of one kind or another is clearly in mind. So why do some scholars express doubts about the burial of Jesus? Should we wonder if he actually was buried? Or, if we believe he was buried, should we wonder if his followers knew where?

In my view, much of the skepticism, not to mention the more speculative and improbable theorizing, is due to lack of familiarity with Jewish burial practices. It may also be due to condescending attitudes on the part of modern scholars and writers of pseudo-history when assessing the narratives of ancient sources. These moderns make unwarranted assumptions about Palestinian Jews of late antiquity, supposing that ascertaining burial locations and maintaining accurate records were either outside the interest of Jesus' contemporaries or beyond their capabilities.

What we shall find is that a review of Jewish burial practices, historical documents from late antiquity, and archaeological data will provide more than sufficient reason to regard the narratives of the New Testament Gospels as informed, credible historical witnesses. The burial of Jesus, as the Gospels describe it, is a datum of history, not a legend or a hoax.

JEWISH BURIAL PRACTICES

The Jewish people buried their dead, then later gathered the bones and placed them in containers called ossuaries or a vault set aside for this purpose. The practice of gathering the bones of the deceased is called ossilegium, or secondary burial (cf. *y. Moe'ed Qatan* 1.5, 80c: "At first they would bury them in ditches, and when the flesh had decayed, they would gather the bones and bury them in ossuaries"). How far back this practice may be traced and where the practice originated are major questions that lie at the heart of the debate surrounding the significance of the numerous ossuaries found in and around Jerusalem, dating to the Herodian period (c. 35 BC–AD 70).

In my view, the most plausible explanation for the dramatic increase in the number of ossuaries put into use in the time of Herod the Great and his successors is Herod's extensive building projects in and around Jerusalem, especially those concerned with the Temple Mount and the new sanctuary. According to Josephus, Herod "prepared a thousand wagons to carry the stones" for the temple and employed "ten thousand of the most skilled workmen," training "some as masons, others as carpenters" (*Ant.* 15.390). The Temple Mount was enormous (and still is) and included a series of buildings and colonnades, with the sanctuary itself the most impressive of all of the structures. Josephus emphasizes the size and beauty of the stones (e.g., *Ant.* 15.399; cf. Mark 13:1: "Look, Teacher, what large stones and what large buildings!"). Although the sanctuary itself and other key structures were completed in Herod's lifetime, work on the Temple Mount continued until AD 64, throughout the respective administrations of his surviving sons, his grandson, and his great-grandson. Accordingly, the meaning of the remark in John 2:20 implies ongoing construction and not completion. It should read: "This temple has been under construction for forty-six years." When work on the Temple Mount was finally completed, Josephus tells us that eighteen thousand workers were laid off (cf. *Ant.* 20.219). This massive layoff contributed to the growing social and political instability that just two years later exploded into open rebellion. Some of the laid-off stone-cutters would later employ their tools and skills in building secret passageways for the rebels (*J.W.* 7.26–27).

It is in this chronological coincidence between Herod's massive building program, which employed thousands of stone-cutters during his reign (in the 30s BC to AD 64), and the appearance of thousands of ossuaries, carved from the same type of stone (limestone) from which almost all of the Temple Mount buildings were fashioned, that we find the answer to our question. The number of ossuaries that were made of limestone increased dramatically during the one century of temple-related building in Jerusalem, not because of a shift in theology or foreign influence, but because of the great number of stone-cutters, quarries, and rejected blocks of limestone. The increase of the city's population and its urban and suburban sprawl also encouraged greater density in burial sites. Simply put, more dead relatives can be interred in the family vault if they are placed in ossuaries than if they are left lying in niches or in full-sized sarcophagi. Although these factors came into play primarily in Jerusalem, their influence may account for the appearance of ossuaries in Jericho and elsewhere during this time.

Now is a good time to review Jewish burial practices of antiquity. First, burial took place the day of death, or, if death occurred at the end of the day or during the night, on the following day. Knowing this lends a great deal of pathos to some otherwise familiar Gospel stories. We think of the story of the widow from the city of Nain: "As he approached the gate of the town, a man who had died was being carried out. He was his mother's only son, and she was a widow; and with her was a large crowd from the town" (Luke 7:12). Her only son had died that day (or the evening before). Her sorrow is at its rawest when Jesus encounters her. We also think of the desperate father, who hurries Jesus to his home, hoping he will arrive in time to heal his dying daughter: "When Jesus came to the leader's house and saw the flute players and the crowd making a commotion" (Matt. 9:23). As it turns out, by the time they arrive, the girl has died and the funeral process, complete with music and weeping, was already under way.

Following death, the body is washed and wrapped. We can find this custom mentioned in several episodes in the Gospels and elsewhere. We see it in the story of Lazarus, who was bound and wrapped with cloths (John 11:44). The body of Jesus is wrapped in a clean linen shroud (Matt. 27:59; Luke 23:53; John 19:40). The body of Ananias is wrapped and buried (Acts 5:6); so also Dorcas, who "became ill and died. When they had washed her, they laid her in a room upstairs" (Acts 9:37). Moreover, the corpse was usually perfumed (Josephus, *Ant.* 15.61; for spices, see *Ant.* 17.196–99; John 19:39–40).

The day of burial was the first of seven days of mourning (*Semahot* 12.1). This is clearly stated by first-century

Jewish historian Josephus, in reference to the death, burial, and funeral of Herod the Great (d. 4 BC): "Now Archelaus [Herod's oldest surviving son] continued to mourn for seven days out of respect for his father—the custom of the country prescribes this number of days—and then, after feasting the crowds and making an end of the mourning, he went up to the temple" (Josephus, *Ant.* 17.200). The custom of seven days of mourning arose from Scripture itself: Joseph "observed a time of mourning for his father seven days" (Gen. 50:10); and, in reference to the remains of king Saul and his sons, Israelite men "took their bones and buried them under the tamarisk tree in Jabesh, and fasted seven days" (1 Sam. 31:13).

Mourning normally took place at the tomb's entrance or within the tomb itself, which is why archaeologists sometimes find a portion of the floor carved out more deeply, allowing mourners to pray standing upright, according to the Jewish custom. Of course, standing inside the tomb was why the corpse was perfumed. Many perfume bottles and jars have been found in tombs and burial caves. One can only imagine how unpleasant the tomb would have become by the sixth and seventh days.

One year after death it was customary to gather the bones and place them in a bone niche or in an ossuary. This practice, sometimes called secondary burial, is readily observed in the archaeological excavations of Jewish tombs in the time of Jesus. It is also attested in later rabbinic literature: "When the flesh had wasted away they gathered together the bones and buried them in their own place" (*m. Sanhedrin* 6:6); "My son, bury me at first in a niche. In the course of time, collect my bones and put them in an ossuary but do not gather them with your own hands" (*Semahot* 12.9; cf. *Semahot* 3.2). The custom of the interval of twelve months from primary burial to secondary burial is also attested in rabbinic literature (cf. *b. Qiddushin* 31b).

For executed criminals, however, the rules were different. Criminals were to be buried properly, but not in places of honor, such as the family tomb. This is clearly taught in the earliest writings of the rabbis: "They did not bury (the executed criminal) in the burying-place of his fathers. But two burying-places were kept in readiness by the Sanhedrin, one for them that were beheaded or strangled, and one for them that were stoned or burnt" (*m. Sanhedrin* 6:5); "Neither a corpse nor the bones of a corpse may be transferred from a wretched place to an honored place, nor, needless to say, from an honored place to a wretched place; but if to the family tomb, even from an honored place to a wretched place, it is permitted" (*Semahot* 13.7). Not only was the body of a criminal not to be buried in a place of honor, no public mourning for executed criminals was permitted: "They used not to make [open] lamentation . . . for mourning has place in the heart alone" (*m. Sanhedrin* 6:6).

The Jewish people believed that the soul of the deceased lingered near the corpse for three days: "For three days (after death) the soul hovers over the body, intending to re-enter it, but as soon as it sees its appearance change, it departs" (*Lev. Rab.* 18.1 [on Lev. 15:1–2]). The change of the face on the third day explains, we are told, why the grief is felt most in the early days of mourning: "The full intensity of mourning lasts up to the third day because the appearance of the face is still recognizable" (*Qoh. Rab.* 12:6 §1). This interesting belief likely lies behind the dramatic story of the raising of Lazarus, brother of Mary and Martha (John 11:1–44). The comments that Lazarus had been dead "three days" and that by now his corpse has "a stench"

(11:39) imply that all hope is now lost. Lazarus has been dead for more than three days. His spirit has departed; his face has changed its appearance. Resuscitation, it was assumed, is no longer possible.

These are the burial customs of the Jewish people. But did the Jewish people always bury the dead? Was burial important to them? Were they willing to leave people, such as executed criminals, unburied?

THE NECESSITY OF BURIAL

In the Mediterranean world of late antiquity, proper burial of the dead was regarded as sacred duty, especially in the culture and religion of the Jewish people. The first reason for providing proper burial was for the sake of the dead themselves. The importance of care for the dead and their proper burial is well attested in Scripture, from the amount of attention given to the story of Abraham's purchase of a cave for the burial of Sarah (Gen. 23:4–19), to the burial accounts of the patriarchs and monarchs of Israel. Of special interest is the story of Jacob's body taken to the land of Canaan, to be buried in a tomb that he had hewn (Gen. 50:4–14). So also Joseph; though buried in Egypt, his bones were exhumed and taken with the Israelites at the time of the exodus, to be eventually buried in Canaan (Gen. 50:22–26; Josh. 24:32). The bones of the slain Saul and sons were buried in Jabesh (1 Sam. 31:12–13). David later commended the men who did this (2 Sam. 2:5: "May you be blessed by the LORD, because you showed this loyalty to Saul your lord, and buried him!"). Saul's bones were later taken to the land of Benjamin (2 Sam. 21:12–14). Even the wicked and divinely judged were buried, too, such as those in the wilderness who

were greedy for meat (Num. 11:33–34), or individual criminals who were executed (Deut. 21:22–23). Israel's enemies,
slain in battle, were buried (1 Kgs. 11:15). Even the eschatological enemy hosts of Gog were to be buried (Ezek.
39:11–16). To leave the dead, even enemy dead, lying about
unburied was to bring a curse on the land (Deut. 21:22–23).

The great importance of proper burial provides the
backdrop for the passages that speak of those who will *not
be buried*, usually because of sin and divine judgment.
Moses warned the Israelites that if they disobeyed the
covenant, their enemies will slay them and their unburied
bodies will be food for birds and animals (Deut. 28:25–26).
Generations later, this judgment befell the families of the
wicked kings Jeroboam (1 Kgs. 14:11) and Ahab (1 Kgs.
21:24). According to the prophetic warning, one from these
families who dies in the city "the dogs shall eat; and anyone
of his who dies in the open country the birds of the air shall
eat" (1 Kgs. 21:23–24). Jezebel herself is eaten by dogs and
becomes "dung on the field" (2 Kgs. 9:33–37); that is, she
has been eaten and then defecated. There will be no marker
that says, "This is Jezebel." Jeremiah warns his own generation with the same disturbing imagery: "The corpses of this
people will be food for the birds of the air, and for the animals of the earth; and no one will frighten them away . . . and
they shall not be gathered or buried; they shall be like dung
on the surface of the ground" (Jer. 7:33; 8:2; cf. 14:16; 16:4;
20:6; 22:19; 25:33; cf. Ps. 79:2–3; Ezek. 29:5; Josephus,
J.W. 1.594: "he would have her body torn to pieces by tor-
ments, and leave no part of it to be buried").

The ghastly image of Jews in exile, murdered and
then left unburied beside the road or flung outside the city
walls, is reflected in the book of Tobit. The book's name-
sake is a righteous man, who observes Jewish food laws,

shares food and clothing with the poor, and buries the dead, even at great personal risk. The theme of Tobit burying the dead may well reflect Jeremiah's earlier warning: Israelites judged and exiled are now murdered and left unburied.

Of all Tobit's virtues, it was his burying the dead that was his greatest (1:18–20; 2:3–8; 4:3–4; 6:15; 14:10–13). Some of the persons whose bodies Tobit buried evidently had been executed by state authority, and not simply murdered. The righteous Tobit explains: "I also buried any whom King Sennacherib put to death when he came fleeing from Judea. . . . For in his anger he put to death many Israelites; but I would secretly remove the bodies and bury [*ethapsa*] them. So when Sennacherib looked for them he could not find them" (1:18). The dead man mentioned in 2:3, whom Tobit also buried, was also executed, either "strangled" (so the NRSV) or "exposed," in the sense of being publicly hanged. This Jewish sense of obligation that Jews executed by Gentile authorities must be buried, even at personal risk, is very significant for the present study.

Josephus's perspective is consistent with that expressed in Tobit. Explaining Jewish ethical obligations, Josephus states, "We must furnish fire, water, food to all who ask for them, point out the road, not leave a corpse unburied [*ataphon*], show consideration even to declared enemies" (*Against Apion* 2.211; cf. 2.205).

Perhaps Philo gives the most eloquent expression to Jewish sensitivities on this question, in his imaginative recounting of Jacob's grief over the report that his son Joseph had been killed and devoured by wild animals. The patriarch laments: "Child, it is not your death that grieves me, but the manner of it. If you had been buried [*etaphes*] in your own land, I should have been comforted and

watched and nursed your sick-bed, exchanged the last
farewells as you died, closed your eyes, wept over your
body as it lay there, given it a costly funeral and left none of
the customary rites undone" (*De Iosepho* 22–23).

The imaginative dirge goes on to speak of the importance of proper burial:

> And, indeed, if you had to die by violence or through
> premeditation, it would have been a lighter ill to me,
> slain as you would have been by human beings, who
> would have pitied their dead victim, gathered some
> dust and covered the corpse. And then if they had
> been the cruelest of men, what more could they have
> done but cast it out unburied and go their way, and
> then perhaps some passer-by would have stayed his
> steps, and, as he looked, felt pity for our common
> nature and deemed the custom of burial to be its due.
> (*De Iosepho* 25)

Jacob concludes his lament by saying that he has experienced no greater tragedy, in that nothing of Joseph remains
and that there is no possibility of burial (26–27). Jewish
sensitivities with respect to proper burial could hardly have
been given more eloquent expression than what we find
here in Philo.

Concern with proper burial continues beyond the
first century. For the Rabbis, burial of the dead was
regarded a sacred duty (cf. *b. Megillah* 3b), taking prece-
dence in the study of the Law, the circumcision of one's
son, or in the offering of the Passover lamb. Indeed, even a
high priest or a Nazirite has the obligation to bury a "neg-
lected corpse," since there is no one else to do it (cf. *Sipre
Num.* §26 [on Num. 6:6–8]).

A second reason for burying the dead is to avoid defilement of the land of Israel. This requirement is grounded in the Mosaic law: "When someone is convicted of a crime punishable by death and is executed, and you hang him on a tree, his corpse must not remain all night upon the tree; you shall bury him that same day, for anyone hung on a tree is under God's curse. You must not defile the land that the LORD your God is giving you for possession" (Deut. 21:22–23). It is also expressed in Ezekiel: "They will set apart men to pass through the land regularly and bury any invaders who remain on the face of the land, so as to cleanse it. . . . Thus they shall cleanse the land" (Ezek. 39:14, 16).

This tradition remained current at the turn of the era, as seen in its elaboration in the Temple Scroll, one of the Dead Sea Scrolls, where we read:

> If a man is a traitor against his people and gives them up to a foreign nation, so doing evil to his people, *you are to hang him on a tree until dead.* On the testimony of two or three witnesses he will be put to death, and they themselves shall hang him on the tree. If a man is convicted of a capital crime and flees to the nations, cursing his people and the children of Israel, *you are to hang him, also, upon a tree until dead.* But you must not let their bodies remain on the tree overnight; you shall most certainly bury them that very day. Indeed, anyone hung on a tree is accursed of God and men, but you are not to defile the land that I am about to give you as an inheritance [Deut. 21:22–23]. (11QT 64:7–13a = 4Q524 frag. 14, lines 2–4, emphasis added)

Whereas Deuteronomy 21:22–23 speaks of one put to death and then hanged, 11QTemple speaks of one hanged "until dead." Most think crucifixion is in view in this latter instance (as also in 4Q169 frags. 3–4, col. i, lines 6–8, and perhaps also in 4Q282i, which refers to the hanging up [probably crucifixion] of those who lead the people astray). This form of execution is notably linked to treason.

It should also be observed that the requirement to bury the executed person on *the day of his death* is emphasized. Deuteronomy simply reads, "You shall bury him the same day," but the Temple Scroll adds, "You must not let their bodies remain on the tree overnight." The reason given for taking the bodies down and burying them the day (or evening) of death is to avoid defiling the land, for the executed person is "cursed of God." This is probably the rationale that lies behind the concern regarding slain enemy soldiers.

In the fragmentary conclusion of the War Scroll, another famous scroll from the region of the Dead Sea, we have reference to the fallen Kittim (i.e., Romans) and their allies. Their corpses lie on the field of battle, unburied. Priests, including the high priest, stand over the corpses and praise God. What is said is not preserved (1QM 19:9–14 = 4Q492 frag. 1, lines 8–13), but it is probable that the priests oversee burial of the corpses and cleansing of the land. The related 4Q285, or Rule of War, which is also fragmentary, supports this interpretation. It seems to say that while Israel celebrates victory over the Kittim (with women beating timbrels and dancing, as in the great victories recounted in Scripture; cf. Exod. 15:20; Judg. 11:34; perhaps also 4Q163 frag. 25, col. iii, lines 1–3), the high priest shall give orders for the disposal of the corpses, evidently to avoid corpse impurity (4Q285 frag. 7, lines 1–6, esp. lines 5–6; cf. frag. 10, lines 4–6: "and you shall eat [the spoil of your enemy . . . and they shall dig] graves for them [. . . and you shall cleanse yourselves from al]l their corpses

. . .". This then explains the meaning in the War Scroll, where it refers to the men who "strip the slain, plunder the spoil, *cleanse the land* . . ." (1QM 7:2–3, emphasis added). Cleansing the land would include burying the corpses of the enemy.

In a section concerned with holiness, the Temple Scroll enjoins Israel: "'For you are a people holy to the Lord your God' [Deut. 14:2]. 'Thus you shall not defile your land' [Num. 35:34]. You are not to do as the nations do: they bury their dead everywhere, even inside their homes. Rather, you must set apart places in your land where you will bury your dead. For every four cities you must designate one burial ground" (11QT 48:10–14). What is important here is that even in the case of the executed criminal, proper burial was anticipated. Various restrictions may have applied, such as being forbidden burial in one's family tomb—at least until the flesh had decomposed—or not being allowed to mourn publicly, but burial was to take place, in keeping with the scriptural command of Deuteronomy 21:22–23 and the Jewish customs that had grown up alongside it.

The commands of Scripture, taken with traditions regarding piety (as especially exemplified in Tobit), corpse impurity, and the avoidance of the defilement of the land, strongly suggest that under normal circumstances (i.e., peacetime) no corpse would remain unburied—neither Jew nor Gentile, neither innocent nor guilty. All were to be buried. What is especially interesting is that some of the tradition reviewed above may have been specifically linked to, even produced by, priests (as in the materials from Qumran). If this is the case, then the relevance of these laws and traditions for the execution of Jesus of Nazareth and its aftermath becomes more evident, for it was the ruling priesthood who

condemned Jesus to death and would have primary responsibility for seeing to the proper burial of his body.

We have reviewed the most important literary evidence concerning Jewish attitudes toward burial. What can
we learn from the archaeological evidence?

THE ARCHAEOLOGICAL EVIDENCE
OF BURIAL IN THE ROMAN ERA

As it so happens, there is significant archaeological evidence that has a direct bearing on the question of whether
the body of Jesus of Nazareth, crucified by order of Pontius
Pilate, was placed in a tomb, as the New Testament Gospels
say it was. As we shall see, the evidence suggests that Jesus
was indeed buried, in keeping with Jewish customs, Roman
tolerance of Jewish customs, and the views expressed by all
Christian and non-Christian literature from late antiquity.
There is in fact not one shred of evidence from antiquity
that suggests Jesus was not buried, which makes it all the
more curious how these ideas and rumors persist.

The important discovery in 1968 of an ossuary
(ossuary no. 4 in Tomb I, at Giv'at ha-Mivtar) of a Jewish
man named Yehohanan, who had obviously been crucified,
provides archaeological evidence and insight into how
Jesus himself may have been crucified. The ossuary and its
contents date to the late AD 20s—that is, during the administration of Pilate, the very Roman governor who condemned Jesus to the cross. The remains of an iron spike
(11.5 cm in length) are plainly seen still encrusted in the
right heel bone (or calcaneum). Those who took down
the body of Yehohanan apparently were unable to remove
the spike, with the result that a piece of wood (from an

olive tree) remained affixed to the spike. Later, the skeletal remains of the body—spike, fragment of wood, and all— were placed in the ossuary. Forensic examination of the rest of the skeletal remains supports the view that Yehohanan was crucified with arms apart, hung from a horizontal beam or tree branch. However, there is no evidence that his arms, or wrists, were nailed to this crossbeam.

The lack of nails or spikes in the hands or wrists of Yehohanan is consistent with a reference in Pliny the Elder (AD 23–79), who refers to rope being used in crucifixion (cf. *Nat. Hist.* 28.4). Nevertheless, it is recorded by others that many victims of crucifixion did have their hands or wrists nailed to the beam. Writing in the second century BC Plautus refers to the crucifixion victim with "his arms and legs . . . double-nailed" (*Mostellaria* 359–61). A third-century AD author described it this way: "Punished with limbs outstretched . . . they are fastened (and) nailed to the stake in the most bitter torment, evil food for birds of prey and grim picking for dogs" (Ps. Manetho, *Apotelesmatica* 4.198–200). One Latin inscription found in Pompeii reads, "May you be nailed to the cross!" (*CIL* IV.2082).

Yehohanan's leg bones were broken, but there is dis-agreement over how and when (i.e., while still on the cross, or after being taken down). Some think that the breaks in the lower leg bones of Yehohanan, including the cut to the talus bone of the foot, are due to *crurifragium*, the breaking of a victim's bones to hasten his death. Others do not think the talus suffered such an injury. Indeed, the talus under question may actually belong to one of the other two indi-viduals whose skeletal remains had been placed in the ossuary. Accordingly, the conclusion that Yehohanan's leg bones were broken before death and decarnation is dis-puted. Because of the age and degraded condition of the skeletal materials, a measure of uncertainty remains.

If Yehohanan's legs were broken before death, we then know not only that he was taken down and buried (as indicated by the discovery of his remains in an ossuary), we also know that his death was intentionally hastened. The most likely and most compelling reason for hastening death in this manner was so that his corpse could be taken down from the cross and placed in a tomb before nightfall, as Scripture commands (Deut. 21:22–23) and as Jewish custom required. The Romans had no reason of their own to expedite death by crucifixion; they would prefer just the opposite.

Also found in the tombs discovered at Giv'at Ha-Mivtar were the remains of a woman who had been decapitated. Whether she was murdered or executed is not clear. (Below I shall give reasons why I think she probably was executed.) However, we may have the skeletal remains of another person who, like Yehohanan, was executed and whose remains eventually were placed in a family tomb. These remains were found in a cluster of tombs on Mount Scopus, north of Jerusalem. In Tomb C the skeletal remains of a woman (aged fifty to sixty) give clear evidence of having been attacked. Her right elbow suffered a deep cut that severed the end of the humerus. Because there is no sign of regrowth or infection, it is surmised that she died from the attack.

In Tomb D, which contains the remains of persons related to those interred in Tomb C, were the remains of a man (aged fifty), who had been decapitated. It is plausible to speculate that this man had been executed, quite possibly for having murdered the female relative in Tomb C. However, physical anthropologist Joe Zias doubts that the man had been executed, because his neck had been struck twice. Being struck twice, he reasons, suggests an act of violence rather than a judicial execution. Zias could be correct, of course, but we should not assume that judicial behead-ings were always neatly done. One only needs to be reminded of the several badly aimed strokes that finally took off the head of James, Duke of Monmouth, in 1685. Apparently the executioner was intoxicated. His first stroke buried the axe in the duke's shoulder! Mary Queen of Scots fared no better a century earlier, when in 1586 her cousin, Elizabeth I, had her executed for treason. It took the execu-tioner three strokes to take off her head.

Forgive me for dwelling on such gruesome data, but I think an important point is to be made here. Multiple cuts, as others might contend, do not in fact argue against interpreting beheadings as judicial executions. I have reviewed the evidence of hundreds of Roman-era skeletons that have been excavated (mostly in Britain, though some in Africa) and have been found to have suffered decapitation. In about one half of the cases two or more strokes of the sword or axe were required before the head was separated from the body.

Of special interest for this topic was the discovery of the mass grave left behind by the bloody battle of Towton, in fifteenth-century Britain. Although dating from a much later period, the skeletal remains are nevertheless quite instructive because the weapons employed and the manner of fighting were essentially the same as those from the ear-lier Roman period. Approximately one half of the several hundred slain had suffered fatal head wounds, and the other half had suffered fatal sword or spear thrusts through the body. Only one victim suffered decapitation, and it may have been a postmortem insult, not the actual cause of death. The point is this: if no one—or at most only one—was decapitated in pitched battle, where combatants were armed with axes and swords, what is the probability that someone suffered decapitation in a domestic altercation? I think it is rather slim.

Accordingly, the man in Giv'at Ha-Mivtar tomb D is probably another individual who suffered the death penalty—even if it took two strokes to finish the job—and whose skeletal remains, in due course, were placed in the family tomb. With all due respect to Joe Zias, I believe this means that we apparently have found three executed persons—one by crucifixion and two by beheading—who were buried according to Jewish customs in the time of Jesus. Thus, they were given primary burial (most likely in a place of dishonor—that is, in one of the tombs reserved for executed criminals) and subsequently their skeletal remains were gathered and placed in ossuaries, which in turn were placed in their family burial vaults, all according to the laws and customs related in ancient Jewish literature.

By the way, if the ossuary bearing the inscription, "James, son of Joseph, brother of Jesus," originally contained the remains of Jesus' brother, then we have one more example of an executed person who was given proper burial, according to Jewish customs. According to Josephus, in the year 62, shortly after the death of Roman procurator Festus, Ananus, high priest and brother-in-law of former high priest Caiaphas, ordered the execution of James the brother of Jesus and a few others (Christians?). When newly appointed Roman procurator Albinus arrived, Ananus was removed from office (*Ant.* 20.197–203). The interesting point is that although James was condemned and executed, he nevertheless was buried.

But why have we found the buried remains of only three or four executed Jews in pre–AD 70 Israel? Surely many more than these were executed. And if other executed persons were buried properly, as I have argued they would have been, then why have we not found many more skeletons of executed persons? Accordingly, it has been argued by some that, in light of the thousands of Jews crucified in the first century in the vicinity of Jerusalem, the discovery of only one properly buried crucifixion victim is proof that the normal Roman practice of not permitting burial must have obtained, even in Jewish Palestine. On the basis of this logic, perhaps one should conclude that Jesus was not buried either.

At least four objections must be raised against this inference. First, almost all of the bones recovered from the time of Jesus are poorly preserved, especially the smaller bones of the feet and hands, which will normally provide evidence, if any, of crucifixion. The presence of the nail in the right heel of Yehohanan made it clear that he had been crucified. The presence of the nail was a fluke. It was due to the sharp end being bent back (like a fishhook), perhaps because the nail struck a knot in the upright beam. When Yehohanan was taken down from the cross, the nail could not be extracted. Accordingly, no statistics should be inferred from this unusual find.

Second, many crucifixion victims were scourged, beaten, and then tied to the cross, not nailed. Thus, skeletal remains would leave no trace of the trauma of crucifixion. Accordingly, we do not know that Yehohanan is the only crucifixion victim discovered in a tomb. For all we know, several other crucifixion victims may have been found without our knowing it.

Third, the best-preserved skeletons are found in the better-constructed tombs, within bone pits or in ossuaries. These tombs were mostly those of the rich, not the poor. The poor were usually buried in the ground, or in smaller natural caves. Not many of their skeletons have been found. The significance of this point is that the poor are most likely to be crucified, not the wealthy and powerful. Accordingly, those skeletons most likely to provide evidence of crucifixion are the skeletons least likely to survive, whereas the best-preserved skeletons are the ones least likely to have belonged to those who had been crucified.

Fourth, the vast majority of the thousands of Jews crucified and left unburied in the first century, in the vicinity of Jerusalem, died during the rebellion of AD 66–70. They were not buried because Rome was at war with the Jewish people and had no wish to accommodate Jewish sensitivities, as Rome normally did during peacetime. It was during peacetime—indeed, during the administration of Pontius Pilate—that both Yehohanan and Jesus of Nazareth were crucified. That both were buried, according to Jewish customs, should hardly occasion surprise. Jewish priestly authorities were expected to defend the purity of Jerusalem (or at least give the appearance of doing so), while Roman authorities acquiesced to Jewish customs and sensitivities, as Philo and Josephus relate.

The archaeological evidence suggests that Jesus and other Jews executed in peacetime Israel were buried, not in honor but properly, in accordance with Jewish laws and customs. In the case of Jesus of Nazareth the expectation would have been to collect his skeletal remains approximately one year after death and transfer them from the place of dishonor to a place of honor, such as his family tomb or burial place. Historical and literary records can tell us more.

BURIAL AND NONBURIAL OF
EXECUTED CRIMINALS IN THE ROMAN WORLD

The objection raised against the Gospels' story of the burial of Jesus rests primarily in the observation that victims of

Roman crucifixion were normally not buried, but their corpses were left hanging on the cross, to be picked apart by birds and animals. That this is the normal Roman practice is not in dispute here. Martin Hengel has assembled most of the pertinent material. A few examples may be cited: "The vulture hurries from dead cattle and dogs and crosses to bring some of the carrion to her offspring" (Juvenal, *Satires* 14.77–78); "the carrion-birds will soon take care of" one's "burial" (Suetonius, *Augustus* 13.1–2); "hanging on a cross to feed crows" (Horace, *Epistles* 1.16.48); and the already cited text that describes the crucifixion victim as "evil food for birds of prey and grim picking for dogs" (Ps. Manetho, *Apotelesmatica* 4.200). On a second-century epitaph the deceased declares that his murderer, a slave, was "crucified alive for the wild beasts and birds" (Amyzon, cave I). Many other texts spare readers such gruesome details, but do mention the denial of proper burial (e.g., Livy 29.9.10; 29.18.14).

What is questioned here, though, is the assumption on the part of a few scholars that the hundreds, even thousands, of Jews crucified and left hanging on crosses outside the walls of Jerusalem, during the siege of AD 69–70, are indicative of normal practice in Roman Palestine. Review of Josephus suggests, to the contrary, that leaving the bodies of the executed unburied was exceptional, not typical. It was, in fact, a departure from normal Roman practice in Jewish Palestine. There is, of course, historical evidence of the failure to bury the executed in some circumstances.

Jews who resisted Antiochus IV (167–164 BC) suffered crucifixion (*Ant.* 12.255–56). We are not told that burial was denied, permitted, or delayed for these persons. However, we should probably assume that normal Jewish burial practice was not permitted by Antiochus, probably to terrorize the Jewish population into capitulation. Two generations later the Hasmonean high priest Alexander Jannaeus crucified some eight hundred of his political opponents, who had allied themselves with Demetrius (*Ant.* 13.380), which is probably what the Nahum pesher mentions (4Q169 frags. 3–4, col. i, lines 6–8). In putting down the revolt following the death of Herod (4 BC), the Roman general Varus crucified two thousand rebels (*J.W.* 2.75; *Ant.* 17.295). Procurator Tiberius Alexander (AD 46–48) crucified the sons of the rebel Judas of Galilee (*Ant.* 20.102). Sometime in AD 52 Quadratus crucified Samaritans and Jews involved in a disturbance during the administration of Cumanus (*J.W.* 2.241; *Ant.* 20.129). The procurator Felix (AD 52–60) crucified a large number of rebels (*J.W.* 2.253). Because of an insult, procurator Florus (AD 64–66) flogged and crucified many in Jerusalem (*J.W.* 2.306). During the siege of Jerusalem (AD 69–70) General Titus crucified Jewish captives and fugitives opposite the walls of the city, to demoralize the rebels (*J.W.* 5.289, 449).

Josephus does not make a point concerning the non-burial of these victims, perhaps because his readers would have assumed that in many of these cases they would receive no burial. Most of these cases involved war or insurrection of one form or another. The cases of nonburial that Josephus does mention all involve murder or execution at the hands of the Jewish rebels. Outraged over the indignity that the rebels practiced on the murdered priests, whose bodies were left unburied, Josephus remarks, "Jews are so careful about funeral rites that even malefactors who have been sentenced to crucifixion are taken down and buried before sunset" (*J.W.* 4.317). Many times Josephus vilifies the rebels, who executed many of the Jewish nobility, by charging that burial of the dead was not permitted, nor even mourning (*J.W.* 4.331, 360, 383; 5.518, 531).

Most of these cases of nonburial involved open rebellion and armed conflict, on the one hand, or mob actions and anarchy, on the other. None of these cases can be said to be normal or typical of peacetime Roman administration. These cases were exceptional and involved desperate attempts to gain or retake control, or terrorize civilian populations. The major difference between Jewish crucifixion and later Roman crucifixion is that in the case of the former the bodies were taken down, at least if they had been crucified in lands inhabited by Jews (cf. Philo, *Flaccus* 83). No corpse in the vicinity of a Jewish city was left unburied at sundown, in keeping with Mosaic law (cf. Deut. 21:23). Moreover, strict Jewish laws regarding corpse impurity, as well as pious devotion to the dead, even criminal dead, would make it unthinkable to leave unburied bodies just outside the walls and gates of Jerusalem.

Peacetime administration in Palestine appears to have respected Jewish burial sensitivities. Indeed, both Philo and Josephus claim that Roman administration in fact did acquiesce to Jewish customs. In his appeal to Caesar, Philo draws attention to the Jews who "appealed to Pilate to redress the infringement of their traditions caused by the shields and not to disturb the customs which throughout all the preceding ages had been safeguarded without disturbance by kings and by emperors" (*De Legatione ad Gaium* 300). A generation later Josephus asserts the same thing. The Romans, he says, do not require "their subjects to violate their national laws" (*Against Apion* 2.73). Josephus adds that the Roman procurators who succeeded Agrippa I "by abstaining from all interference with the customs of the country kept the nation at peace" (*J.W.* 2.220).

The actions of Herod Antipas, with respect to John the Baptist, are consistent with this policy. Although the Baptist is executed by the tetrarch, his disciples are nonetheless allowed to bury his body (Mark 6:14–29; Josephus, *Ant.* 18.119).

Even Roman justice outside the Jewish setting sometimes permitted the crucified to be taken down and buried. We find in the summary of Roman law (known as the *Digesta*) the following concessions:

> The bodies of those who are condemned to death should not be refused their relatives; and the Divine Augustus, in the Tenth Book of his *Life*, said that this rule had been observed. At present, the bodies of those who have been punished are only buried when this has been requested and permission granted; and sometimes it is not permitted, especially where persons have been convicted of high treason. (48.24.1)
>
> The bodies of persons who have been punished should be given to whoever requests them for the purpose of burial. (48.24.3)

The *Digesta* refers to requests to take down bodies of the crucified. Josephus himself makes this request of Titus (*Life* 420–21). Of course, Roman crucifixion often did not permit burial, request or no request. Nonburial was part of the horror—and the deterrent—of crucifixion. But crucifixion—during peacetime—just outside the walls of Jerusalem was another matter. Given Jewish sensitivities and customs, burial would have been expected, even demanded.

The evidence thus far reviewed strongly encourages us to think that in all probability Jesus was indeed buried and that his corpse and those of the two men crucified with him would not have been left hanging on the cross overnight and perhaps indefinitely, or at most cast into a ditch or shallow grave to be exposed to animals. Quite apart from any concerns with the deceased men or their families, the major concern would have had to do with the defilement of the land and the holy city. Politically, too, it seems unlikely that on the eve of Passover, a holiday that celebrates Israel's liberation from foreign domination, Pilate would have wanted to provoke the Jewish population and incite Jewish nationalism. Moreover, it is equally improbable that the ruling priests, who had called for Jesus' death, would have wanted to appear completely indifferent to Jewish sensitivities, either with respect to the dead or with respect to corpse impurity and defilement of the land. It seems most probable that the priests would have raised no objections to the burial of the three men. Indeed, they probably would have arranged to have them buried, before nightfall, in tombs reserved for executed criminals, which is what is actually stated in the Mishna (cf. *m. Sanhedrin* 6.5–6) and in the New Testament Gospels, with respect to Jesus.

THE BURIAL OF JESUS

In the early 1900s, Kirsopp Lake argued that the followers of Jesus knew that their master had been buried; they just did not know where. Lake famously proposed what has become known as the Wrong Tomb theory, in which the story of the resurrection of Jesus is explained away. According to this theory, we are to believe that the women who looked on as the body of Jesus was placed in a criminal's tomb returned the following Sunday morning to a similar but wrong tomb. Finding it unoccupied and misunderstanding the words of a helpful young man (proposed to be "His is not here; he is up there"), the frightened and confused women ran away and told the disciples about their strange experience. From this report the disciples concluded that Jesus must have been raised from the dead. How the followers of Jesus could be so inept and so gullible is not explained.

Other intriguing alternative theories also have been proposed. One is dubbed the Swoon Theory, whereby it is suggested that a wounded and comatose Jesus was placed in a tomb, a few days later awakened, somehow extricated himself, and then found his way to his startled disciples, creating in them the impression that he had been resurrected and glorified. Why his disciples would have viewed a seriously injured, limping Jesus in such terms is not clear. And, of course, we have been taxed with a series of conspiracy theories, from Hugh Schonfield's *The Passover Plot* to Michael Baigent's silly *The Jesus Papers*.

All of these alternative theories stumble over archaeological and literary evidence, mostly having to do with Jewish burial traditions. Suggestions that Jesus' followers would not be able to find the correct tomb in which their master had been interred or that a still living Jesus would be buried and then, awakening, could actually manage to exit the tomb and be perceived by anyone in any way other than what he was—a badly injured man in need of medical attention—have not impressed qualified historians and archaeologists. The conspiracy theories are even more ludicrous, not only unable to explain how it is that such a grotesque secret was kept by so many, but also unable to discover a cogent motive for such a caper in the first place.

The recent claim that a tomb in East Talpiot, located between Jerusalem and Bethlehem (excavated in 1980), was the tomb of Jesus and his family throws the discussion into a whole new light. The proponents of this view have no doubts that Jesus was properly buried. What is remarkable is that they believe the family tomb of Jesus and the very ossuary that at one time contained his skeletal remains have been found.

However, there are also many problems with this theory, and I am not aware of any competent archaeologist who agrees with it. Perhaps the most demonstrably false claim in the East Talpiot Tomb hypothesis is the claim that the pointed gable with circle over the tomb's entrance is an early Jewish-Christian symbol, which is said to lend important support to the claim that the tomb really did belong to the family of the founder of the Christian movement. This interpretation of the pointed gable and circle symbol is completely erroneous. On the contrary, this symbol suggests that the occupants of the tomb in all probably numbered among the very people Jesus offended, who would have called for his death.

The pointed gable over a circle or rosette is seen in other tombs and ossuaries, some of which predate the Christian era and none of which are believed to have anything to do with Jesus and his movement. We see this artistic design in the outer and inner façades of the so-called Sanhedrin Tombs in Jerusalem. Over the inner entrance of this tomb complex one can see the pointed gable over a rosette, comprising acanthus leaves. A gable is also found over the outer entrance, but without rosette. This pattern is seen in the Hinnom Valley Tomb, the Tomb of Jehoshaphat, and the so-called Grape Tomb.

In various books concerned with archaeology and Jewish symbols one can find several photographs and facsimiles that depict the gable and circle or rosette. Among these items are ossuaries, a tomb façade, a coin (struck by Philip, tetrarch of Gaulanitis in the time of Jesus), and epitaph art. One of the more common features is the Torah Ark (which contains Scripture scrolls), over which the pointed gable and circle appear. Scholars have remarked that Jewish funerary art often incorporated imagery influenced by the Herodian temple and often depicted with point gable and circle or rosette. Excavations of the Jewish tombs of Beth Shearim in Galilee have uncovered the same artistic motifs. Again we find a Torah Ark, at the top of which is the gable above a circle (or rosette), painted on a sealing stone.

The gable and circle or rosette pattern is found on several ossuaries, with the circle or rosette on the end of the ossuary, over which rests the gabled lid, or on the end of the lid itself, thus forming the very pattern seen over the entrance to the East Talpiot Tomb. An ossuary found on Mount Scopus is particularly relevant, for it depicts monumental façades, with temple motifs, on all four sides. Both ends and one side present pointed gables over entrances. Beneath two of these pointed gables (on one end of the ossuary and on the less finished side of the ossuary) is a circle, in a pattern quite like what we see over the entrance to the East Talpiot Tomb.

Finally, depictions of the Torah Ark, complete with gable and circle (or rosette) are found in synagogue art. Striking examples are found in the art adorning the walls of the Dura Europos synagogue, where the designs are in reference to the Jerusalem temple.

The evidence is overwhelming, and what has been surveyed above is but a sampling. The conclusion that should be drawn is quite clear: The pointed gable and circle over the entrance to the East Talpiot Tomb is Jewish and has nothing to do with Jesus and early Christians. The symbol is probably in reference to the temple. Given the fact that aristocratic and high priestly families were buried in the greater Talpiot area (among them possibly the family of Caiaphas, former high priest) and the fact that every single name in the East Talpiot Tomb is Hasmonean, it is probable that this tomb belonged to a wealthy, aristocratic Jerusalem family with ties to the Jerusalem temple. Indeed, some of the members of the family buried in the East Talpiot Tomb may have been ruling priests. The suggestion that the gable and circle adornment over the East Talpiot Tomb constituted an early Christian symbol has no foundation and ignores a mountain of contrary evidence.

The proponents of this theory are correct in thinking that Jesus' body would have been buried, in keeping with Jewish customs. But they are completely mistaken in thinking his bones and ossuary, along with those of other members of his family, would have been placed in a high-quality tomb, in the neighborhood of other tombs containing the remains of aristocratic Jews, adorned with a symbol proclaiming temple and priestly affiliation.

SUMMING UP

The literary, historical, and archaeological evidence points in one direction: the body of Jesus was placed in a tomb, according to Jewish custom. Furthermore, there is no good reason to think that family and friends of Jesus had no idea where Jesus was buried or had no plans eventually to recover his skeletal remains and transfer them to his family tomb or to another place of honor.

In view of the evidence, I believe the burial narratives of the New Testament Gospels deserve a fair reading. If their respective reports are coherent and if they accord with known literary and archaeological evidence, then they should be accepted. In my opinion much of the skepticism that has been voiced is not particularly critical and often reflects ignorance of the Jewish burial traditions that this chapter has taken pains to review.

The Gospels tell us that "Pilate . . . granted the body to Joseph . . . and laid it in a tomb" (Mark 15:42–46). According to Jewish law and custom, the executed criminal could not be buried in his family tomb. Instead, his body was to be placed in one of the burial vaults set aside for such persons (cf. *m. Sanhedrin* 6:5–6; *Semahot* 13.7). There it must remain, until the flesh has decomposed. One rabbinic text addresses this point, specifically in reference to someone who has been crucified: "If one's (relative) has been crucified in his city, one should not continue to reside there. . . . Until when is one so forbidden? Until the flesh is completely decomposed and the identity unrecognizable from the bones" (*Semahot* 2.13). Because the Jewish Council (or Sanhedrin) delivered Jesus to the Roman authorities for execution, it was incumbent upon it to arrange for proper burial (as in *m. Sanh.* 6:5 cited above). This task fell to Joseph of Arimathea, a member of the council. The Gospel narrative is completely in step with Jewish practice, which Roman authorities during peacetime respected.

The Gospels tell us that "Mary Magdalene and Mary the mother of Joses saw where the body was laid" (Mark 15:47). It was necessary for Jesus' family and friends to observe the place where the body of Jesus was placed, for it was not placed in a tomb that belonged to his family or otherwise was under their control. The reburial of the bones of Yehohanan, the man who also had been crucified under the authority of Pontius Pilate, demonstrates that the Jewish people knew how to note and remember the place of primary burial. The family and friends of Jesus anticipated recovering his skeletal remains, perhaps one year later, so that they "may be transferred from a wretched place to an honored place," as the law allowed (cf. *Semahot* 13.7; *m. Sanh.* 6:6).

Jesus was placed in the tomb Friday afternoon. The first opportunity for anyone to visit the tomb, during daylight hours, was Sunday morning. The Gospels tell us that "Mary Magdalene, and Mary the mother of James, and Salome bought spices, so that they might go and anoint him. And very early on the first day of the week, when the sun had risen, they went to the tomb" (Mark 16:1b–2). The women's intention to anoint the body of Jesus indicates their intention to mourn for their master in the tomb itself. In the cases of executed criminals, private mourning was allowed. As has already been mentioned, the spices were to be used to perfume the corpse, in order to mask the unpleasant odor.

As the women approach the tomb, they ask, "Who will roll away the stone?" (Mark 16:3). Matthew says a guard was posted, to prevent the removal of Jesus' body (Matt. 27:65–66). We probably should assume that the evangelist has referred to the custodian, whose placement in the vicinity of the tombs set aside for executed criminals was to see that burial laws were not violated. The most serious of these laws was the prohibition against moving a body from a place of dishonor to a place of honor. The guard or custodian would also enforce the prohibition against public mourning for an executed criminal.

In view of Jesus' status as a criminal and in view of the presence of a guard (perhaps reinforced because of the popularity of Jesus), the women knew that there would be

reluctance to assist them in rolling back the stone that covered the opening of Jesus' tomb. They also knew that even
their combined strength probably would not be sufficient
to roll the stone aside. Study of the skeletal remains from
this period of time indicates that the average woman was
barely five feet tall and often weighed less than 100 pounds.
The average man was five feet four inches and weighed 135
pounds. Sealing stones weighed hundreds of pounds. Even
round stones, which were designed to be rolled aside,
would have been very difficult to move. The Markan evangelist, moreover, comments that the stone was very large
(Mark 16:4b). Accordingly, the women wonder where they
might find assistance. Two of the best-known Jerusalem
tombs with circular sealing stones and grooved tracks are
the Tomb of the Family of Herod and the Garden Tomb
(also known as Gordon's Tomb).

According to the Gospels, when the women arrived
at the tomb of Jesus, "They saw that the stone . . . had
already been rolled back" (Mark 16:4). The statement that
the stone was "rolled back" implies a round stone over the
entrance to the tomb. In Jewish Palestine of late antiquity,
80 percent of the doors were square; only 20 percent were
round. Discovery of the opened and empty tomb would
have dismayed the women, especially Mary, the mother of
Jesus, when reported to her, for this would mean that the
body of Jesus had apparently been relocated. Jesus had
died on Friday, so Sunday was the third day of death.
According to Jewish tradition, the face of the corpse was no
longer recognizable on the fourth day. Therefore, the
women knew that if Jesus' body was not found *that day*,
then it probably would never be identified and therefore
could not be claimed and transferred to his family tomb at
some future date. Their interpretation of what they saw that

Sunday morning was informed by Jewish burial customs, not an expectation of Jesus' resurrection.

When all pertinent data are taken into account, we have every reason to conclude that Jesus was properly buried the very day of his death. He was taken down from the cross before nightfall and was buried according to Jewish customs (Mark 15:42–16:4; 1 Cor. 15:4). Jesus was put to death as a criminal, and he was buried accordingly (*m. Sanh.* 6:5; *Semahot* 13.7). The novel suggestion that perhaps Jesus was left on the cross, unburied (as was usually the case outside Israel; cf. Suetonius, *Augustus* 13.1–2; Petronius, *Satyricon* 111), or that his corpse was thrown into a ditch, covered with lime, and left for animals to maul, is wholly implausible. Obligations to bury the dead properly, before sundown, to avoid defiling their sacred land, were keenly felt by Jews of late antiquity.

Further, it is very probable that some of Jesus' followers (such as the women mentioned in the Gospel accounts) knew where Jesus' body had been placed and intended to mark the location, perfume his body, and mourn, in keeping with Jewish customs. The intention was to take possession of Jesus' remains, at some point in the future, and transfer them to his family burial place.

The discovery of the opened tomb and the absence of Jesus' body threw the women into confusion and set the stage for a surprising and completely unexpected experience. This surprising experience is addressed in chapter 3.

FURTHER READING

Brown, R. E. "The Burial of Jesus (Mark 15:42–47)." *Catholic Biblical Quarterly* 50 (1988): 233–45.

Evans, C. A. *Jesus and the Ossuaries: What Jewish Burial Practices Reveal about the Beginning of Christianity.* Waco, TX: Baylor University Press, 2003.

McCane, B. R. "'Where No One Had Yet Been Laid': The Shame of Jesus' Burial." In *Authenticating the Activities of Jesus.* Edited by B. D. Chilton and C. A. Evans, 431–52. New Testament Tools and Studies 28.2. Leiden: Brill, 1998.

Meyers, E. M. *Jewish Ossuaries: Reburial and Rebirth.* Rome: Pontifical Biblical Institute, 1971.

Toynbee, J. M. C. *Death and Burial in the Roman World.* Ithaca, NY: Cornell University Press, 1971.

Chapter Three

THE SURPRISE OF RESURRECTION*

N. T. Wright

The resurrection remains controversial today, even among
Christians. This is partly because, in my experience at both
the scholarly and the popular level, many Christians today
use the word "resurrection" very loosely, to mean something
that it did not mean in the first century. It is often used today
simply as a somewhat exalted way of talking about "going to
heaven when you die." Many books about the resurrection
end up being all about the glorious future that awaits immediately beyond the grave, rather than the ultimate future and
resurrection itself. Additionally, I have observed that many
Easter sermons go at once from the fact of Jesus' resurrection to the fact of the Christian hope, seen not in terms of
bodily resurrection but in terms of a glorious life after death
in some disembodied heaven. (The day before I edited this
piece for publication, I attended a funeral in which, at point
after point, all these confusions were on display; if someone
was there who had not known before what classical
Christianity believed about the ultimate promised future,
the liturgy would have left them deeply confused.)

---

*A fuller presentation of the arguments outlined here can be found in two other books
by N. T. Wright: in chaps. 3 and 4 of *Surprised by Hope: Rethinking Heaven, the
Resurrection, and the Mission of the Church* (London: SPCK, 2007/San Francisco:
HarperOne, 2008), which is itself based on the arguments that are extensively outlined
in *The Resurrection of the Son of God* (London: SPCK/Minneapolis: Fortress, 2003).

All this ignores a rather obvious fact: the word "resurrection" never did mean "disembodied bliss." Furthermore,
in the New Testament itself, the word "resurrection" does
not mean "life after death." It meant, and means, what I call
"life *after* life after death." Although this is quite a difficult
idea for some to get a hold of, if you go back to the ancient
world, whether pagan or Jewish, the word "resurrection,"
along with its various cognates in other languages, is clearly
not a way of talking about the destiny of people immediately
after death. It is a way of referring to a newly embodied life
at some time beyond that point. The simplest way to see this
is to think of Jesus' words to the brigand on the cross:
"Today you will be with me in Paradise" (Luke 23:43). But,
as Luke makes clear, Jesus wasn't raised until Sunday.
"Paradise" must therefore refer to the place, or state, of bliss-
ful waiting *before* the bodily resurrection.

THE LANGUAGE OF "RESURRECTION"
IN THE ANCIENT WORLD

The pagan world denied resurrection itself, even though
many pagans believed in all kinds of different theories
about life after death. The one thing they knew did *not* happen was people coming back into a bodily life at some point
after death. There is a famous story in Greek mythology of
Orpheus and Eurydice that illustrates the point. Eurydice,
Orpheus's beloved, had died and gone down to Hades,
existing in a shadowy form in the underworld. Orpheus
was then allowed to go down and seek permission to bring
Eurydice back up again, but with this stipulation: if he
looked back to see her while leading her out of Hades,
which he naturally was longing to do, then he would lose

her and she would be gone forever. So they start the journey up the long, ascending stairway, but eventually Orpheus's longing to see his beloved gets too strong and he looks back, therefore losing her permanently. (I recently read a feminist poem in which Eurydice was trying to flirt with Orpheus, teasing him to make him look back, because the last thing she wanted was to be saddled with having a man in her life again. I suspect that was not what the original mythographers had in mind!) The point of the myth is clear: you can think about what it might mean if somebody were to come back bodily from the dead and really be here again in some significant bodily way, but the pagan world knew it did not actually happen. This same sort of denial of bodily resurrection is also there in Homer, Plato, and Pliny, and it is there consistently through a thousand years of paganism, up to and through the time of Jesus.

The Jewish world, by contrast, did hold out the possibility of resurrection, which can be observed in some of the later Old Testament writings, especially in a passage like Daniel 12. This text speaks of the righteous or the martyrs waiting until the time when many, who sleep in the dust of the earth, will awake, arise, and shine like the stars. Daniel 12 was very significant for later Jewish thinkers and writers. They went back to it again and again, to say that after "life after death" (which is a period of being asleep, resting, or waiting), there will be a new bodily life either for the righteous, or for the martyrs, or perhaps for all God's people. In fact, for some Jews, as for many early Christians, the belief was that every single human being who had ever lived would be raised bodily from the dead in order to face their maker and be judged for what they had done in the body. There would be no point judging a disembodied soul for the things the body had done. For others—this varies from text to text—the "resurrection" itself is reserved only for God's people.

Before embarking on a study of "resurrection," then, we need to get straight right from the beginning what the word "resurrection" was all about. To start with the negative, "resurrection" was not a fancy way of talking about a beautiful, glorious life after death. Rather, it always was a way of talking about a further life after a period of being dead. When the Christians said that Jesus was raised from the dead on the third day, they must have meant this; otherwise, why was he not raised from the dead immediately upon his death itself? Why wait for three days? However, many theologians and writers in the last century have tried to argue that this is not what the Christians really meant. They contend that the early Christians really meant that Jesus had died and gone to heaven in some exalted fashion, and that they then started to use the terminology of resurrection for it, ultimately inventing stories on that basis. In one of my books, *The Resurrection of the Son of God*, I have taken up this point in much greater detail. In that book, among other things, I have dealt with every single contemporary argument that I have been able to find on the whole subject. In the end, I have found that the question of Jesus' resurrection has been muddled up with various other issues that are perceived to be related to it, but are actually not that relevant at all.

THE METHOD AND MADNESS OF HISTORICAL STUDY
OF THE RESURRECTION STORIES

As I come and go to America and lecture in various places, I have discovered a phenomenon that we do not have in

Britain. Americans have a clear polarization, both politically and theologically, between what you could broadly call "liberal" and "conservative." One of the things that Marcus Borg and I have enjoyed, when debating in public, is that people attempt to typecast us as "liberal" and "conservative," when really neither of us fits those categories nearly as well as people think we will. In fact, as I look at the issues I see all kinds of blurring of lines. There is, for instance, a pressure on many people in North America to take on the label "liberal" in order to prove that they are not one of those wretched fundamentalists, or perhaps to take on the label "conservative" in order to prove that they are not simply followers of Bishop Jack Spong (to name but two stereotyped examples). This is neither a mature nor a helpful way of doing theology or biblical studies, or indeed of living wisely within society. But these pressures and tendencies often become bound up with questions about miracles, questions about the Bible, questions about the supernatural and other similar things. When you mention any of those issues, you can feel the room divide. For the purpose of our present enquiry, all those knee-jerk reactions need to be put on hold: what we need to do in examining Jesus' resurrection is not to react to our contemporary pressures but to engage in historical inquiry. We must examine what exactly happened on the first Easter day. Coming with a bunch of a priori assumptions or political or theological commitments from our own culture, whether East or West, British or American or whatever, is not a legitimate way of doing history.

Some will at once contend, however, that historical inquiry about the resurrection is extremely puzzling. As soon as you read Matthew, Mark, Luke, and John side by side, challenges seem to arise. It is difficult to tell which women went to the tomb on Easter morning. It is not clear how many journeys they made to and fro. It is unclear whether Peter and John both went as well or just Peter at least to begin with. Additionally, questions remain: Who saw Jesus first and when? Did Jesus mostly appear in Galilee or mostly in Jerusalem, or some of both? Though these questions are not quite as difficult as some have made out, there are plenty of problems when you try to sort through them.

I have another example of an analogous situation or problem from the mid-twentieth century, which illustrates the kind of thing we are dealing with. There was a wonderful moment on October 25, 1946, when the then two greatest philosophers in the world met for the first and only time. Ludwig Wittgenstein and Karl Popper came face to face because Wittgenstein was chair of a philosopher's group in Cambridge, and Popper was coming to deliver a paper to that group. They gathered in somebody's large study in Cambridge. There was a fire burning in the grate, and next to it was a poker. Wittgenstein picked up the poker and waved it around as he was making a point to Popper. Suddenly, Wittgenstein threw down the poker and left the room. Popper had not expected any of this, though people who knew Wittgenstein well were not surprised by this sort of behavior even in an academic setting.

Within only weeks, rumors had gone around the world that Popper had been threatened by Wittgenstein with a red-hot poker, yet, all the great minds who were present, including Bertrand Russell and many other household names in the world of philosophy, law, and other disciplines, could not agree on what exactly had happened and in what order. Did Popper make a crushing rejoinder before Wittgenstein left the room, or did he make a key comment only afterward? At what point did Wittgenstein pick up the poker? Was it hot or cold? Did he slam the door or did he leave quietly? A wonderful book came out some years ago called *Wittgenstein's Poker* (London: Faber, 2001), written by two enterprising journalists, David Edmonds and John Eidinow, who have gone into this incident in great detail. They have come up with a hypothesis about what actually happened, which fits a bit closer to some of the accounts and not quite so closely to some of the others. They deconstruct and discredit Popper's own account, on the grounds that he had a self-serving reason to tell the story in terms of his scoring a famous victory over Wittgenstein, which probably wasn't really the case. So there was continuing disagreement, but we should notice that nobody would say that nothing at all happened—that there was not a meeting, that there was not a poker, that there were not two philosophers, and that one of them did not leave the room. Something happened, but it was so dramatic, so quick, and so unexpected that all of the eyewitnesses, who were all people professionally concerned with the pursuit of truth, never quite agreed. As any lawyer will know, this is often what you find when people give eyewitness evidence. Exciting and dramatic things often happen, but eyewitnesses disagree about them. However, to reemphasize, that does not mean that nothing happened. Rather the reverse. This, I believe, is what we should conclude from our puzzled initial readings of the Gospel stories.

EARLY CHRISTIAN DISTINCTIVES ON RESURRECTION

Now, when we come to early Christianity, and we plot early Christian beliefs about life after death and resurrection on the same map as ancient pagan beliefs and ancient Jewish beliefs, we find several very interesting things. Beliefs about life after death are notoriously one of the more conservative things in a culture. People may change their minds about other aspects of what they believe, but what they believe about death (including what they believe about how you should do funerals) tend to be pretty conservative. People may be exploratory in other aspects of their worldview, but when somebody they love dies they want to do a funeral pretty much like the funerals they always knew. With the early Christians, who came from every corner of Judaism and every corner of paganism, you might well have thought that over the first two centuries we would find evidence of all sorts of beliefs about life after death held by different Christian groups. The extraordinary thing is that we do not. From Paul, on through the New Testament, through the Apostolic Fathers and through the great theologians at the end of the second century (e.g., Irenaeus, Tertullian, and Origen), we find a remarkably consistent set of beliefs about what will happen to God's people ultimately after death.

A notable exception to this remarkably consistent picture of early Christian belief about resurrection appears in the writings that we call Gnostic (e.g., the Gospel of Thomas). These writings, which have been much vaunted in some contemporary American scholarship, are some-times hailed as very early and as giving access to the original Christian vision that was then muddled up by the later New Testament writers, not least by the four canonical evangel-ists. I have argued at some length for the opposite view on these writings, namely that the Gnostic writings are late, and that they derive from and indeed deviate from the canonical writings. This is actually the majority view of New Testament scholars around the world, though you might not know that in North America just now. In the end, these writings are best seen as reflecting a later attempt to use the language of early Christianity, in this case in talking about life after death, to express a radically different worldview.

The early Christian worldview at this time was seriously Jewish, rather than pagan. When we ask where the early Christians belong on the map of the history of religions, they clearly are to be seen as a mutation from within Judaism. Even when they are going out on the street in Corinth and Ephesus, even when they are sailing off to Rome and elsewhere, even when everybody in the church seems to be an ex-pagan rather than an ex-Jew, the worldview and beliefs they hold, as well as the kind of life they are trying to live, is recognizably Jewish in kind. However, there are seven modifications within the Jewish belief about resurrection that the early Christians introduced and to which they all subscribed to a lesser or greater extent.

The early Christians held firmly to a view of a future hope that focused on resurrection. They did not simply believe in a life after death in some platonic sphere, where the righteous souls go off to heaven after death and, in good platonic bliss, get to talk philosophy all day. The early Christians seldom actually speak about going to heaven when they die. Search through the New Testament and you find scant evidence of any such thing. There are passages that speak about "going to be with Christ" in this interim period (e.g., Phil. 1:23). There is Jesus' promise to the brigand dying beside him, that they will be together in Paradise that very day (Luke 23:43). And there is Jesus' famous promise about the "many dwelling places" prepared in his father's house (John 14:2). But, again and again, the focus is not where you will be instantly after death. The focus is on where you will be in God's new world, in the new creation, in the new heavens and the new earth. The answer given is that, in that world, you will be a newly embodied self. The early Christians held firmly, as did the Pharisaic Jews, to a two-step belief about the future: first an interim waiting period, and second a new bodily existence in a newly remade world. Let me stress again, there is nothing like this in paganism.

Another pertinent preliminary remark concerns the contemporary assumption that we moderns, since we live in a scientific age, know in a new way that dead people do not come back to bodily life again. This is really nothing more than an absurd piece of Enlightenment rhetoric. Everybody in the ancient world knew that when people were dead, they stayed dead. Even those Jews who believed in resurrection did not expect it to happen earlier on. Martha's response to Jesus at the raising of Lazarus reflects this. She fully associates Lazarus's rising with the resurrection on the last day, not now (John 11:24). This current misunderstanding of what we know as opposed to what people in the ancient world knew expresses itself in the assumption that we now know "the laws of nature" and that people before the eighteenth century basically did not. On this idea, C. S. Lewis once tartly remarked that the reason Joseph was worried about Mary's pregnancy was not because he did not know where babies came from but because he did. The ancient world was not ignorant. Some like to make out that it was, but in fact they knew a whole lot back then. We must beware of a kind of chronological snobbery, an assumed superiority to our ancient forebears.

The early Christians articulated their belief in resurrection within this very Jewish system of belief, but not without some significant alterations or mutations. We can track seven of these.

The first mutation is that within early Christianity there is virtually no spectrum of belief about resurrection. There are a few local variations: at the end of Revelation, we have a double resurrection, which exegetes continue to puzzle over; in Hebrews, we certainly have a mention of the resurrection, but it does not seem to be as developed as in some of the other early Christian writings. But still this does not even approach the breadth of the spectrum of views on life after death that we see within paganism. Nor does it even reflect the more limited variety of belief in Judaism (not all Jews went with the Pharisees on resurrection). In early Christianity, there basically is no variety of belief to be charted.

The second mutation is similar: resurrection is not as important a belief in Second Temple Judaism as it is in early Christianity, where it is central and vital. If you look at the Rabbis, it is apparent that they believe in resurrection. Yet, apart from one or two discussions, the voluminous rabbinic tomes are concerned mostly with other things. The space and significance devoted to resurrection does not compare with the space given to other topics. When one goes to the Dead Sea Scrolls, it is still possible to make the argument that the Qumran writers did not even believe in resurrection. Though I join with others who cautiously make the argument that they did, most will still agree that resurrection is not a big topic in Qumran. It is hardly ever mentioned. Yet for the early Christians it is absolutely central.

To see just how central it is, consider this fact. In many debates today between "conservatives" and "liberals," the two primary points over which people argue are the virgin birth and the empty tomb. Yet within the New Testament this is a distortion. The virgin birth, though important, is not nearly as vitally important to the Gospels as resurrection. You can take the birth of Jesus away and you lose a chapter at the beginning of Matthew, two chapters at the beginning of Luke, and that is about it. But try taking the resurrection, the bodily resurrection, out of the New Testament, and watch how one argument after another collapses to the ground. The same is true for the Christian writings in the generations after the New Testament was written. Consider, for instance, what happened in AD 177. The martyrs of Lyons, in southern France, were killed not least because the pagans could not stand them going on about the resurrection. When the Christians were burned to death, the pagans declared that they would burn their bodies and then scatter the ashes in the river so that they would never be able to have a resurrection. Resurrection went on being crucial and vital, and was one of the key things the church was known and persecuted for. Galen, the great second-century doctor from Asia Minor, which we know as Turkey, says he only knows two things about the Christians: one, that they believe in resurrection, and two, they show remarkable sexual restraint. It is very interesting and telling that public perception of this strange new group included an identification of their resurrection belief. Resurrection in early Christianity is thus central and vital, far more so than within Judaism.

The third early Christian mutation within Second Temple Jewish belief about resurrection is a much more detailed view of what precisely resurrection means. If you look at Second Temple Jewish texts, you can see some like 2 Maccabees 7, where it really appears as though resurrection is going to mean simply coming back into a body very much like this one. But, if you go to Daniel 12, it says that the righteous will shine like stars. In the Jewish writing called 2 Baruch, we can see how some writers are taking this up, so that these resurrected beings are almost like angels, though still emphatically bodily. In early Christianity, by contrast, we have much more precision about what sort of a body the resurrection body will be. The answer is that it will be a transformed body. It will still be a material body, but it will have significantly new properties.

Paul is the one who sets this out most clearly. Unfortunately, though, the passage in which he does this is one of the most misunderstood in all his writings. In 1 Corinthians 15, he speaks of the present body and the future body, and he describes them both in some detail. Sadly, in the RSV and in the NRSV translations of the Bible, exactly the wrong sort of adjectives are used to translate Paul's two key phrases. What Paul refers to as the present body and the future body, the RSV and NRSV translate as "physical body" and "spiritual body," respectively (1 Cor. 15:44). So a whole generation—perhaps more—of English readers in Britain and North America have assumed that for Paul the resurrection was not "bodily" in the sense of "physical." Therefore, they say, for Paul there was no empty tomb; nothing actually happened "physically" because it was a purely "spiritual" event. In *The Resurrection of the Son of God* I have argued, based on the actual Greek words used, the history of those words, the structure and meaning of Paul's argument in this passage, and what Paul says elsewhere in his writings on the same topic, that these are simply and clearly mistranslations. If we today say "physical" and "spiritual," we are bound to hear those words in terms of the platonic distinction between the material world of space, time, and matter on the one hand and something on the other hand that is more like a ghost or a spirit—something that you cannot see or touch but which you may be aware of in a kind of extrasensory way. That is precisely not what Paul is talking about.

Two points sustain this. First, the sort of adjectives that he is using here are not ones that describe the sort of thing something is made of. They are adjectives that describe the sort of thing that is *animating* something. To illustrate, suppose someone sees a ship out in the harbor somewhere and wonders, "Is that a steel ship or a wooden ship?" That question would concern the sort of thing that it is made of. But these adjectives in Paul are more like the person asking, "Is that a steam ship or a nuclear-powered ship?"—in other words, asking about what is driving the ship, what is animating it. That second kind of adjective, the one that refers to the animating force or principle, is the kind of adjective Paul is using here. The distinction he is making is not, then, between "physical" and "spiritual" in our sense. The distinction he is making is between a body, a "physical" body in our sense, that is animated by normal human energy (a "natural" body, in other words), and the new body which will be animated by God's spirit, in other words, a "spiritual" body in the sense of a spirit-generated and spirit-animated body.

You can see this very clearly in Romans 8:9–11, which is actually the clearest statement from Paul on this whole topic. There Paul declares, "If the Spirit of him who raised Jesus from the dead dwells in you, he who raised Christ from the dead will give life to your mortal bodies also through his Spirit that dwells in you." There is no doubt what Paul is talking about there. It is new life for the mortal body, not a new life away from the body. So, for example, when Paul says flesh and blood cannot inherit God's kingdom (1 Cor. 15:50), he does not mean that what we call "physicality" cannot inherit God's kingdom. He is talking about the *present* physical body, which is corruptible and will decay and die, and a *future* body that will be incorruptible and that will be incapable of decaying and dying. For Paul the phrase "flesh and blood" does not mean simply physicality; it means corruptibility, decaying, and dying. It is hard for us to imagine a noncorruptible state of physicality, but that is what Paul says the new creation will be.

We should note, however, that this transformed physicality, or "transphysicality" as I have called it elsewhere, does not involve being transformed into luminosity. Here people again make a very easy interpretative mistake. They assume that when Paul is talking about "glory," he means shining like an electric lightbulb. He usually does not. There may be one or two passages when Paul is moving in that direction, perhaps with echoes of Daniel 12, but more often that text is used by Paul metaphorically of Christians witnessing in the world. In Philippians, Paul uses it not in order to say that we will be shining like a light, but in order to say that our witness, the holiness of our lives, will shine out, in that metaphorical sense, into the world (Phil. 2:15). So the third mutation within the Jewish view of resurrection is that we see much more clearly what this body will be like. It will be a transformed physicality: not that it will be shining, but that it will be incorruptible, incapable of decaying or dying. This emphasis goes through from Paul to Irenaeus and beyond.

The fourth surprising point or mutation in the Christian view of resurrection is that the resurrection, as an event, has split into two. Jews who believed in resurrection believed that it would occur on the last day when God made the new heavens and new earth. It would happen to everyone altogether. Nobody ever imagined that this final event would be anticipated in the case of one person in the present. No first-century Jew, prior to Easter, expected it to be anything other than that large-scale, last-minute, all-people event. That is why, when Jesus tells the disciples not to tell anyone about the transfiguration until the Son of Man is raised from the dead (Mark 9:9), they are very puzzled, because for them "this rising from the dead" (9:10) was not something that was going to happen to one person, leaving the rest of them in a position to go about telling people what they have just witnessed. "The resurrection," as far as they were concerned, ought to have been something happening to everybody, at the end. There were of course other Jewish movements, which had some sort of "inaugurated eschatology," that believed God had already begun to fulfill his promises, but none of them claimed that resurrection itself had already happened to one particular person; and that, of course, was precisely what the early Christians did claim. And they went on claiming it; and they redefined and revised the Jewish way of telling the story of God, Israel, and the world, to take account of the fact that God's new creation had already begun. That, today, is one of the key points for Christians to grasp when we think about the significance of Easter.

The fifth remarkable modification from within the Jewish belief is that the early Christians developed a quite new metaphorical use of "resurrection." Ever since Ezekiel 37 and the story of the valley of dry bones—that great vision of the bones coming together and standing up on their feet and God's breath entering into them—resurrection language could be used as a metaphor for the restoration of Israel, the return from exile, the new exodus. It was a way of saying that God was going to do an astonishing feat of restoring the fortunes of his people. Now we must notice that the Jews who used resurrection language in that *metaphorical* sense also continued to use "resurrection" in the *literal* sense, referring to the new embodiment that would happen to God's people at the end of time. This (to put the point the other way round) didn't stop them using it in this metaphorical sense, to talk about something that might happen before that, namely the return from exile or the great restoration. Fascinatingly, in early Christianity that particular metaphorical use has disappeared virtually without trace, with only one little line (in Rom. 11:15) that might conceivably be seen as an echo of it. In its place we have a different metaphorical use of resurrection, as early as Paul and going into the early Christian tradition. Resurrection language is used metaphorically to describe baptism and holiness. It is used metaphorically, but without damaging the full literal meaning, because the early Christians still believed in a literal resurrection at the end, based on the literal bodily resurrection of Jesus. Nor does the new metaphorical usage refer simply to an abstract entity, to a state of mind, a state of heart, or a type of spirituality. The fact that it is metaphorical does not stop it from referring to concrete events: baptism and holiness, after all, are concrete things that actually happen to your body. So there has been a transformation of the Jewish metaphorical language of resurrection at that point.

The sixth modification of the Jewish resurrection belief was its association with messiahship. At that time, nobody expected that the Messiah would be raised from the dead, for the simple reason that nobody expected that the Messiah would be killed in the first place. This was a totally new thing, and it leads us to reflect just a little bit on how impossible it is to account for the early Christian belief in Jesus as Messiah unless something like the resurrection took place. Often people fail to think historically at this point, so let us just indulge in a little serious historical thinking. Several other Jewish messianic or prophetic movements took place in the first century. One of the best known was during the Jewish-Roman wars of AD 66–70 when the leader—whom many of the Jews regarded as their true leader, king, and possibly the Messiah—was a man called Simon bar Giora. Simon bar Giora was taken back to Rome in order to be paraded through the streets as part of Titus's triumph. At the end of Titus's triumph, as Josephus describes it, Simon was ceremonially killed. He was flogged and then executed, which was how the Romans carried these things out. As has been described so well in chapter 1, it was much more satisfying to have the enemy king killed in public at the height of your triumph than simply buried under rubble somewhere back in Jerusalem.

Imagine, then, the situation of some of Simon's followers who had somehow escaped capture. Supposing one of them said, two or three days later, "Simon really was the Messiah." The others would almost certainly say, "What on earth do you mean? What are you talking about? The Romans got him. They killed him. Of course, he isn't the Messiah. Everybody knows that it is the job of the Messiah to defeat the pagan enemy, to rebuild the temple, and to bring God's justice to the world. Instead, he has been defeated by the pagans; the temple is in ruins; God's justice is nowhere to be seen. All we have is Roman justice, thank you very much." In response, suppose then the friends said, "Oh, no. You see, I think Simon has been raised from the dead." The others would likely say, "Well, that is extremely odd. What do you mean? There is no sense of that in our Scriptures. What are you talking about?" If then in clarifying (and I am here following the kind of line of thought that dozens and dozens of New

Testament scholars this last century have tried to advance), the friends had then said, "Oh, no, I don't mean that he has been bodily raised, leaving an empty tomb behind. I mean that I have had a sense of his presence with me. I have had a sense that the cause for which he fought is still going forward. I have had a sense that God has forgiven us for running away and leaving Simon to his fate." Now, if the others were feeling kind, they might say, "Well, my dear fellow, you have been sitting in the sun a bit too long." Or, they might say, "Well, it seems like you have had some kind of interesting spiritual experience. We Jews, as you know, have a tradition of singing psalms, reading the prophets, and offering special prayers when we have special kinds of experience. Why don't you do that? Why are you saying he has been raised from the dead? He clearly hasn't been; he's still dead and buried; and if he hasn't been raised then he certainly wasn't and isn't the Messiah."

You see, after Jesus of Nazareth had been executed, anybody two days, three days, three weeks, or three years after that would never have said he was the Messiah, unless something extraordinary had happened to convince them that God had vindicated him—something grander than simply going to heaven in some glorious exalted state. That is what they believed had happened to the martyrs. They had ways of talking about that. They would almost certainly have said that he *would be* raised from the dead in the future. They would never have said that this had already happened.

Had Jesus' followers wanted to carry on with the messianic movement after Jesus' movement had failed with his own death, they had an option: find another Messiah. There are some groups in Judaism who did that in the first century. Each time a would-be Messiah got killed, the movement found another one, perhaps his brother, his cousin, his nephew, or his son. Now observe: The great leader in the early church was James, the brother of the Lord. He was the great respected figure, a man of prayer, a fine teacher. He was respected not only by the Christians but also by the Jewish authorities. Everybody knew he was the brother of Jesus. Yet nobody dreamed of saying that James was the Messiah. They should have done so, according to this pattern, unless for the very good reason that they believed Jesus himself really was the Messiah, and the only reason that you would believe such a thing about someone who had been crucified was that he had been raised from the dead.

To round off this sixth mutation: because of the early Christian belief in Jesus as Messiah, we find the development of the very early belief that Jesus is Lord—and therefore that Caesar is not. As early as Paul, the resurrection of Jesus—and the future resurrection of all his people—is the foundation of Christian allegiance to a different king, a different Lord. Resurrection was not, and is not, a soft way of talking about death itself. It isn't a matter (as some have suggested) of some people "interpreting 'death' as 'resurrection.'" "Resurrection" is a way of saying that death is overthrown, and with that overthrow, the power of those who depend on it has gone. Despite the sneers and slurs of some contemporary scholars, it was those who believed in the bodily resurrection who were being thrown to the lions and burned at the stake for the next three centuries. Resurrection was never a way of settling down and being respectable. It may function like that in some parts of Britain, North America, and elsewhere today, working as part of a "conservative" package that supports the status quo in politics or theology. It certainly didn't function like that in Judaism or in early Christianity. It was the Gnostics who translated the language of resurrection into private spirituality and dualistic cosmology. It was the Gnostics who escaped persecutions. It was the Christians who found themselves persecuted again and again. Resurrection means making the public claim about Jesus that challenges other public constructs of reality, other political as well as spiritual powers.

The seventh and final mutation within the Jewish belief in resurrection is what Dominic Crossan has called "collaborative eschatology." With the resurrection of Jesus, the early Christians believed not only that God had begun the long-awaited new creation, but that he had enlisted them, through the spirit of Jesus, as helpers within that project. After Easter, new creation isn't simply something the Christians waited for. It is something in which they were called to help. This is a massive theme, but there is no space to explore it further at this point.

FOUR STRANGE FEATURES OF THE RESURRECTION STORIES IN THE GOSPELS

I have given over a great deal of space to these "mutations" within the Jewish view of resurrection, partly because I have discovered that they are not widely known, and partly because they are necessary if we are to understand the Easter stories themselves. We must now look at these stories, and at four strange features of them in particular, which, once again, frequently go unnoticed.

First, as we read the Easter stories, we note the strange absence of Scripture in them. When you read the Gospel accounts of Jesus' last days—of his arrest, his trial, and his crucifixion—you find Old Testament echoes, quotations, and allusions all over the place. The Psalms, Isaiah,

Daniel, Zechariah, and other books have provided material that has then been woven into the structure of the narrative. Turn over the page to the Easter accounts, and what has happened to all that scriptural allusion and echo? It is just not there. John tells us that the two disciples who went to the tomb "did not yet know the scripture that he must rise again from the dead," but he does not tell us which Scripture he is talking about. Luke has Jesus expound the Scriptures to the two on the road to Emmaus, but even in that story he never actually quotes or mentions one of them. This is extraordinary because, as early as Paul (e.g., 1 Cor. 15) we can see a very sophisticated hermeneutic of several biblical texts already firmly embedded in early Christian theology. But in these Gospel narratives there is no mention of particular passages, scarcely even an echo of the Old Testament.

One could suggest, I suppose, that this scriptural absence has come about because the people who wrote down those narratives in the second generation had gone through the stories and taken out all of the biblical allusion and echo. That won't work when we have four independent narratives telling the story in different words and different ways. It is much more plausible to argue that these stories, though written down later, actually reflect the very, very early, prereflective eyewitness accounts in which people had not even begun to wonder whether or not this strange set of events fulfilled certain Scriptures. They were, it seems, too eager to tell their friends and neighbors and families the extraordinary things they had just seen and heard. I therefore regard that as one piece of evidence indicating that the stories, though written down later, must go back to very early oral tradition fixed in that form. Once you tell a story like that (and believe me, if you had experienced something like that, you would tell it over and over again), the story would very quickly acquire a fixed form, just as when you repeat an anecdote two or three times you tend to settle down into one particular way of telling it. Though the resurrection stories have been lightly edited by the different evangelists, they reflect quite closely four of the ways in which that story was told right from the start.

The second strange feature of the resurrection stories is the presence of women as the primary witnesses. Whether we like it or not, women were simply not regarded as credible witnesses in the ancient world. Now when the tradition had time to sort itself out, as we see reflected in the first paragraph of 1 Corinthians 15, the women have been quietly dropped. When it came to public apologetics, in that world, it would have been very embarrassing to think that your main witnesses to this extraordinary event were women, not least someone with the extraordinary reputation of Mary Magdalene. But there they are in all four Gospel stories, front and center: the first apostles, the first people to tell others that Jesus was raised from the dead. In concert with what is noted earlier in this book, it is simply incredible to suppose that the tradition began with the male-only form that we find in the tradition Paul quotes in 1 Corinthians, and then developed, in significantly different ways, into the four female-first stories we find in the Gospels. Here again, the stories really do look as if they are very, very early.

The third strange feature, which goes with the third modification of the Jewish resurrection belief, is the portrait of Jesus himself. Many people have tried to make out over the last century that the Gospel stories developed in the following manner. First, people after Jesus' death were so overcome with grief that they really did not know what they were thinking. Second, they gradually acquired a new spiritual consciousness, a new belief that Jesus' cause continued. Third, from this new religious experience, they gradually started to explore the Scriptures. Fourth, from this they then (and only then) started to use the language of resurrection to articulate their experience. Finally, toward the end of the first century, some people began to invent stories about an actual resurrection, which the early church had never envisaged. Capping this proposed progression of thought is the idea that, in Luke and John (which are supposed on this theory to be the last Gospels to be written, perhaps toward the end of the first century), people were so concerned to stress that Jesus really was a real physical being, a real embodied being, that they invented stories about him eating broiled fish, cooking breakfast by the shore, being able to be touched, and so on.

The problem is that this proposed development is very strange, even in Jewish terms. If the early Christians had gone this route, searching the Scriptures and inventing stories on that basis, you would have expected them to envisage the risen Jesus shining like a star. That, after all, is what the popular text in Daniel 12 says about people being raised from the dead. They do not. They describe him like that in the transfiguration, for whatever reason, but none of the resurrection stories even hint at that. Indeed, Jesus appears as a human being with a body that is like any other body; he can be mistaken for a gardener, or a fellow traveler on the road. In addition, the stories also contain definite signs that the body has been transformed. Nobody, I suggest, would have invented them just like this. The body is clearly physical. It has, so to speak, used up the matter of the crucified body—hence the empty tomb. But, equally, it comes and goes through locked doors; it is not always recognized; and eventually it disappears altogether into God's space (which is how we ought to think of "heaven").

This kind of account is without precedent. No biblical text predicts that the resurrection will involve this kind of body. No speculative theology laid this trail for the evangelists to follow, and to follow in such interestingly different ways. In particular, this should put a stop to the old nonsense that suggests that Luke's and John's accounts, which are the most apparently physical, were written late in the first century in an attempt to combat Docetism—the view that Jesus was not a real human being but only seemed to be. Granted, if all you had was Jesus eating broiled fish and inviting Thomas to touch him, we might have thought that Luke and John were trying to say, "Look! He was really a solid physical person!" However, those very same accounts are the ones in which Jesus appears and disappears, passes through closed doors, and finally ascends into heaven. These stories are extremely peculiar, and the type of peculiarity they possess is not one that would have been invented. It looks as though the Gospel writers are struggling to describe a reality for which they didn't really have adequate language.

The fourth and final strange feature of the resurrection narratives, which may call into question many of the Easter sermons that I and others regularly preach, is the absence of any mention of the future Christian hope. Almost everywhere else in the New Testament, where you find people talking about Jesus' resurrection, you find them also talking about our own future resurrection, the final hope that one day we will be raised as Jesus has been raised. But the Gospels never say anything like, "Jesus is raised, therefore there is a life after death" (not that many first-century Jews doubted that there was); or, "Jesus is raised, therefore we shall go to heaven when we die" (most people believed something like that anyway); or better, "Jesus is raised, therefore we shall be raised at the last." No: insofar as the event is interpreted in Matthew, Mark, Luke, and John, it has a very "this-worldly" meaning, relating to what is happening here and now. "Jesus is raised," they say, "therefore he is the Messiah; he is the true Lord of the whole world; therefore we, his followers, have a job to do: we must act as his heralds, announcing his lordship to the entire world." It is not, "Jesus is raised, therefore look up into the sky and keep looking because one day you will be going there with him." Many hymns, prayers, and Christian sermons have tried to pull the Easter story in that direction, but the line of thought within the Gospels themselves is, "Jesus is raised, therefore God's new world has begun, and therefore we, you, and everybody else are invited to be not only beneficiaries of that new world but participants in making it happen."

SO WHAT REALLY HAPPENED AND
HOW CAN WE KNOW IT?

There is much more to say about the Gospel resurrection narratives, but I want to come now to the conclusion and climax by addressing briefly the question: what then can we say about what happened, and how we can know about it? I begin with what I regard as fixed historical points. The only way we can explain the phenomena we have been observing is by hypothesizing two things: first, that Jesus' tomb was really empty; second, that the disciples really did encounter him in a way which convinced them that he was not simply a ghost or a hallucination. Some additional elaboration on these two points is in order.

Hypothetically, let us suppose that the disciples had seen, or thought they had seen, someone they took to be Jesus. This would not, by itself, have generated the stories we now have. Everyone in the ancient world took it for granted that people had strange experiences of encountering dead people. They knew at least as much as we do about visions, ghosts, dreams, and the fact that when somebody is grieving over a person who has just died, they sometimes see, briefly, a figure that seems to be like that person appearing to them. This is not a modern invention or discovery; ancient literature is full of it. They had language for that sort of phenomena, and that language was not "resurrection." They described these situations as a kind of angelic experience.

Acts 12 exemplifies this. Here, Peter is in prison, and the disciples are having an all-night prayer meeting, praying for his safety, because Herod wants to kill him. Then, astonishingly and miraculously, Peter is let out of jail and he comes to the house where the Christians are praying. He knocks on the door—and they are so full of faith that they cannot believe it is actually him! Rhoda, the maid who goes to answer the knock on the door, is so excited that she forgets to open the door, and she runs back announcing that Peter is outside. Those gathered respond by saying she is out of her mind, but she insists it really is him. They then posit that it must be his "angel." What do they think has happened? They think Peter has been killed in prison and that this is that kind of postmortem visitation of an angelic, shadowy, "spiritual" figure. They think it must be a figure like Peter, or representing Peter, paying them a quick visit to say goodbye. This would be perfectly compatible with going to the prison the next day in order to take Peter's body away and give it a decent burial. In other words, however strong those experiences of meeting someone like Jesus might have been, without an empty tomb people would have said it must have been his "angel." Yet they do not. They say he has been raised from the dead—that he is no longer dead, but alive.

Equally, had there been just an empty tomb, with no sightings of Jesus, that would have proved nothing. Grave robbery was common. With soldiers, guards, and political enemies, all sorts of explanations would have been possible. Some would have gone at once for those explanations, had not the empty tomb been accompanied by sightings of and meetings with Jesus himself.

Some time ago, when I was writing my book on resurrection, a friend came to see me unexpectedly and asked what it was about, and I told him "resurrection." Straightaway, he said, "Oh, of course I have always taken the view that the idea of resurrection was in the air at the time, and the disciples were so bothered by Jesus' cataclysmic defeat and death that they more or less reached for that category as a way of coping with their grief." That is totally implausible as a historical account of something that happened in the first century. We know, as I said before, of several other movements where the leader was killed, the one upon whom everyone had pinned their hope; but at no point do we find such movements then suffering from the blessed twentieth-century disease called cognitive dissonance, where they make up stories about something glorious that has happened in order to try to come to terms with their grief. That just doesn't work as history.

Likewise, the account offered by many theologians all the way from Rudolf Bultmann to Edward Schillebeeckx will not do. Schillebeeckx contended that when the disciples went to the tomb their minds were so filled with light that it did not matter whether there was a body there or not. At that point, Schillebeeckx has simply stopped being a first-century historian and has become a twentieth-century fantasist. Folk in the first century knew plenty about people's minds being filled with light. They had language for that. They had the psalms. They had traditions of spirituality. But this had nothing to do with saying that someone had been raised from the dead.

People often lodge complaints here, saying that this kind of discussion seems overly concerned with "facts," and so much of religious language is actually about metaphor and about faith. Well, it is of course true that religious language does necessarily use metaphor, and that faith remains central. But the point about Judaism and Christianity is that they are focused on creation; that is, they believe in a God who made the world of space, time, and matter and who wants to reclaim it. Thus, what happens in the real world actually matters. If somebody came off the street and accused the church treasurer of running off with the money, it would not do to say, "Did you mean that in some metaphorical sense?" We would want to know, did he do it or didn't he? An important part of learning to read Scripture is that when we find a parable, we treat it as a parable. The "truth" of the parable of the Prodigal Son does not depend on our being able to prove that something like that actually happened. Yet it is an equally important part of learning to read Scripture that, when the writers intend to express something that actually happened, we do not treat it as a parable. The "truth" of the crucifixion story would be totally undermined if it could be proved that Jesus died of pneumonia in Galilee, even though of course the crucifixion sets off all kinds of metaphorical resonances in the minds of people ancient and modern. And the "truth" of the resurrection story is like that too. If it didn't happen, it isn't true. The fact that the truth of Jesus' resurrection sets off its own resonances in the worlds of metaphor and symbol doesn't mean that it can be reduced to those resonances. We have to learn both of those skills, not only one: how to read parables as parables, and how to read historical narrative as historical narrative.

All this brings us, then, face to face with the ultimate question. The empty tomb and the meetings with Jesus are, I believe, solidly established as historical data. They are the only possible explanation for those Easter stories, and for those mutations in the Jewish beliefs that grew up so quickly. How then do we explain this data? Historians often explain by means of inference to the best explanation. If I am an archaeologist and I find in an archaeological site two pillars of a certain type and design that have distinct patterns, and notice indications that maybe an arch had previously joined the two pillars; if, then, I look in my textbooks and I see that pillars like that normally had this kind of arch; and, if I am so fortunate to dig further and find an arch exactly like the one in the book—the same measurements and all—then I say, the game is over, this hypothesis works, these pillars really did support an arch. We infer to the best explanation: it really was this arch that sat on top of those pillars.

Now, though this does not amount to actual "proof" of Jesus' resurrection, I contend that, after having studied all the other possible arches that scholars have proposed which might join the two pillars (the empty tomb and the sightings of Jesus), there is nothing that comes remotely near explaining these phenomena, except for the following proposal: Jesus of Nazareth really was raised from the dead on the third day, leaving an empty tomb behind him, and being raised into a newly embodied state where he had gone through death and out the other side into new bodily life *after* his brief "life after death." Of course, the stories have the same surface inconsistencies as the stories of *Wittgenstein's Poker*, but that is just the way that eyewitness stories are. This does not mean that nothing happened. On the contrary, it means that what happened was so powerful and dramatic that it instantly generated excited and perhaps confused retellings.

Again, I do not claim that this amounts to (as it were) a mathematical proof of Jesus' resurrection. Some theologians get very twitchy about this, and imagine that if you appeal to Enlightenment historiography to tell you what happened at Easter, you are treating Enlightenment historiography as God, and forcing everything else to fit in with it. I am not doing that here. We are faced at this point with issues of worldview, and on such matters there is no such thing as neutral ground. Historical argument alone cannot force anyone to believe that Jesus was raised from the dead. But historical argument is remarkably good at clearing away the undergrowth behind which skepticisms of various sorts have been hiding. The proposal that Jesus was bodily raised from the dead possesses unrivaled power to explain the historical data at the heart of early Christianity. The obvious fact that this remains hugely challenging at worldview levels—challenging personally, socially, culturally, and politically—ought not put us off from taking the question very seriously.

Finally, on a wider note, I have become convinced that the climate of skepticism, which has for the last two hundred years made it unfashionable and even embarrassing to suggest that Jesus' resurrection really happened, was never and is not now itself a neutral position sociologically or politically. The Enlightenment achieved a kind of intellectual coup d'état that convinced many people that we somehow had new evidence for the fact that dead people do not rise—as though this was a modern discovery, rather than simply the reaffirmation of what Homer and others took for granted. That proposal, that coup d'état, goes hand in hand with the other things the Enlightenment asserted, not least the proposal that we have now come of age; that we do not need God anymore; that God can be kicked upstairs into a kind of deistic heaven; and that religion and spirituality consist of the flight of our aloneness to God's aloneness, so that we can then get on running the world down here and carving it up to our own advantage without interference from beyond. This was the proposal of the Enlightenment. The denial of the bodily resurrection of Jesus went with that social, cultural, and political agenda.

To that extent, the totalitarianisms of the last century were simply among the varied manifestations of a larger totalitarianism of thought and culture against which post-modernity has now decisively rebelled. Who after all was it who did not want the dead to be raised? It was not simply the intellectually timid or the rationalists. It was, and is, those in power: the social and intellectual tyrants and bullies; the Caesars who would be threatened by a Lord of the world who had defeated death, the tyrant's last weapon; the Herods who would be horrified at the postmortem validation of the king of the Jews. It brings to mind Oscar Wilde's wonderful scene in his play *Salome*, the play that Richard Strauss used as the basis for his opera of the same name. In that play Herod hears reports that Jesus of Nazareth has been going around healing people and raising the dead. Herod is quite happy to have Jesus healing people. He quite likes the idea of somebody doing healings, but he is horrified at the thought that Jesus is raising the dead. Herod responds by saying, "I do not wish him to do that. I forbid him to do that. I allow no man to raise the dead. This man must be found and told that I forbid him to raise the dead." Here we see the bluster of the tyrant who knows that his power is threatened. I hear the same tone of voice not just in the politicians who want to carve up the world to their advantage but in the intellectual traditions that have gone along for the ride. Wilde's next line, though, is the real crunch, for us as for Herod. "Where is this man?" demands Herod. The courtier replies, "He is in every place, my lord, but it is hard to find him."

FURTHER READING

Segal, Alan F. *Life after Death: A History of the Afterlife in Western Religion*. New York: Doubleday, 2004.

Wright, N. T. *The Resurrection of the Son of God*. Christian Origins and the Question of God. Vol. 3. London: SPCK/Minneapolis: Fortress, 2003.

———. *Surprised by Hope: Rethinking Heaven, the Resurrection, and the Mission of the Church*. London: SPCK, 2007/San Francisco: HarperOne, 2008 (esp. chaps. 3–4).

INDEX OF ANCIENT SOURCES

INDEX OF SUBJECTS, NAMES, AND PLACES